"Alice Keeler and Matt Miller provide a foundation for any educator looking to make a pedagogical shift in their classroom and ditch the homework. The book leaves readers with ideas to start in their school the next day, such as ways to build relationships with students, effective feedback techniques, and real-world learning opportunities using suggested tools and strategies. Most importantly it reminds educators that we do not teach to a one-size-fits-all community, and educators need to remember to have empathy and offer equitable learning experiences that engage and empower students within the classroom. Students then might be driven to continue their work at home, discovering their passions along the way."

—RAYNA FREEDMAN, INSTRUCTIONAL TECHNOLOGY SPECIALIST AND MASSCUE PRESIDENT-ELECT (@RLFREEDM)

"Every day I talk to more educators and parents who are becoming convinced that homework isn't a good way to spend kids' time out of school. *Ditch That Homework* provides real-world ways to get off the homework train by working bell-to-bell and maximizing time in class, not sluffing off things to worksheets and word searches that don't benefit anyone academically."

—JON CORIPPO, CUE CHIEF INNOVATION OFFICER (@JCORIPPO)

"*Ditch That Homework* is not just a book about *why* educators and parents should rethink homework, but it's a practical guidebook for how to do things differently. Matt and Alice have filled this book chock-full of resources for educators, kindergarten and up, who want to begin or continue their journey toward ditching homework. As a parent of a young school-aged child, this book left me feeling empowered and inspired to continue to support the shift towards making homework obsolete."

—KARLY MOURA, TEACHER ON SPECIAL ASSIGNMENT (@KARLYMOURA)

"Matt and Alice have done it again! They've written a book that I'll come back to time and time again for resources, ideas, and suggestions I can use to make my classroom a better place for students! When we take the time to build relationships and create authentic and engaging learning experiences for our students, it results in a community of lifelong learners who are curious, insightful, and excited to come to school each day! *Ditch That Homework* explicitly shows educators how they can make their class time *so* effective and efficient that homework and other traditional practices will no longer be necessary!"

—**Paul Solarz**, FIFTH-GRADE TEACHER AND AUTHOR,
Learn Like a PIRATE (@PaulSolarz)

"Wow! Thank you for helping educators to rethink homework and equipping them to challenge the status quo of classrooms by providing practical ways to be more efficient, effective, and purposeful with what we do. The resources, strategies, and ideas mentioned in *Ditch That Homework* are simple, doable shifts that are exactly what is needed for today's classroom that should be used even if your goal isn't to ditch homework."

—**Sean Fahey**, SIXTH-GRADE MATH TEACHER (@SEANJFAHEY)

"*Ditch That Homework* is a tremendous resource that will help classroom teachers teach better. It encourages a shift toward practices that benefit all students, not just compliant students. Matt and Alice have provided many ideas to transform how students can practice and learn without sending work home. *Ditch That Homework* will help build relationships with students, help teachers grade less but provide more feedback, and help families reclaim time together."

—**Mandi Tolen**, HIGH SCHOOL MATH TEACHER
AND GOOGLE INNOVATOR (@TTMOMTT)

"*Ditch That Homework* is a transformational book for teachers who are working towards the *no-homework* classroom. Matt and Alice have a very easy conversational style to 'talk' with the reader and support the teacher as you make your way through this astounding collection of resources to support making this change. In addition, Matt and Alice share various pieces of evidence to understand why the no-homework classroom allows students to grow the most as people and also as learners. Best of all, Matt and Alice share examples of how to make this happen in your classroom."

—**KRISTA HARMSWORTH**, FIFTH-GRADE TEACHER (@ZONIE71)

"Homework can be a sensitive topic; however, it has been proven to not show any benefit to student learning. Through brain research, pedagogical examples, and family values, Matt and Alice offer up applicable reasons for ditching homework. Teachers will frequently return to this book for countless resources and to ensure they're serving their students in the most beneficial student-centered, homework-less environment."

—**EVAN MOSIER**, TECHNOLOGY INTEGRATIONIST (@EMOSIER3)

"An engaged classroom built on solid relationships, meaningful work, conversations, and a push for creativity doesn't require tasks outside of class. It is the educator's responsibility to create an optimal learning environment for students to learn and want to *continue* to learn. Alice and Matt give an overview of why ditching homework is a sound practice and provide a practical, comprehensive map to get us there. Even if you only use a fraction of the ideas, your class, parents, and your students will benefit!"

—**LANCE McCLARD**, ELEMENTARY PRINCIPAL (@DRMCCLARD)

"Matt and Alice hit a homerun with this one—better yet, a grand slam! I've been a no-homework advocate since my first year of teaching. It's a passion of mine that stems from limited support at home as a little girl. *Ditch That Homework* is a strong foundation to support educators as they weather the storms of resistance. In fact, Matt and Alice beautifully paint *why* it's imperative we rethink the 'way we've always done it' mentality regarding homework. As if the research and testimonials aren't convincing enough, Miller and Keeler generously hand the reader an overabundance of strategies necessary to execute no homework, system wide. While this is a *must-read* for all educators, I want each member of our administrative team to have a copy. It's vital for the entire system to embrace the content of this book; our students deserve it!"

—TARA MARTIN, DISTRICT ADMINISTRATOR, CURRICULUM COORDINATOR, AND #BookSnaps FOUNDER (@TaraMartinEDU)

"Imagine your instruction is so effective that you don't need to assign homework! Alice and Matt provide practical ideas and resources to do just that. Learn why and how to finally ditch homework."

—CRAIG KLEMENT, INSTRUCTIONAL COACH (@CRAIGKLEMENT)

"Matt and Alice have really approached a hot topic with honest and open experiences about the inequities they have experienced with homework! A practical guide, whether you're a novice or veteran teacher, to give resources and guide in the transformation of your teaching. Challenging the ideals of conventional practice to truly reach the whole child and re-light that spark in learning!"

—ANNE KAMPER, INSTRUCTIONAL COACH (@AnneKamper)

"*Ditch That Homework* is a game changer! Alice and Matt build a compelling case around why we should reconsider–and ultimately ditch–giving homework. More than just theory, *Ditch That Homework* is also a practical guide for teachers. Each section is rich with resources to explore, and Alice and Matt provide countless strategies, ideas, and tools for how to engage students and use in-class time more effectively. My toolbox is bursting! I highly recommend this to educators of all grade levels. It's time we set our students' personal lives free and let go of the age-old tradition of homework!"

—RACHEL MARKER, K–8 CURRICULUM SPECIALIST (@RACHELMARKER)

DITCH THAT HOMEWORK

PRACTICAL
STRATEGIES TO
HELP MAKE
HOMEWORK
OBSOLETE

MATT MILLER AND ALICE KEELER

Ditch That Homework

© 2017 By Matt Miller and Alice Keeler

This book is available at special discounts when purchased in quantity for use as premiums, promotions, fundraisers, or for educational use. For inquiries and details, contact the publisher at books@daveburgessconsulting.com.

Published by Dave Burgess Consulting, Inc.
San Diego, CA
http://daveburgessconsulting.com

Cover Design by Genesis Kohler
Editing and Interior Design by My Writers' Connection

Library of Congress Control Number: 2017943781
Paperback ISBN: 978-1-946444-39-4
eBook ISBN: 978-1-946444-40-0

First Printing: July 2017

CONTENTS

INTRODUCTION xi
The Homework Paradox

CHAPTER 1 1
Ditch That Textbook

CHAPTER 2 17
Ditch That Lecture

CHAPTER 3 39
Ditch That Referral

CHAPTER 4 55
Ditch That Resistance

CHAPTER 5 71
Ditch Those Habits

CHAPTER 6 85
Ditch That Remediation

CHAPTER 7 119
Ditch That Compliance

CHAPTER 8 139
Ditch That Red Pen

CONCLUSION 153

ACKNOWLEDGMENTS .157

REFERENCES 158

MORE FROM DAVE BURGESS CONSULTING, INC. 162

BRING MATT MILLER TO YOUR SCHOOL,
DISTRICT, OR EVENT! 173

ABOUT THE AUTHORS .175

INTRODUCTION
The Homework Paradox

> Every child is an artist.
> The problem is how to remain
> an artist once we grow up.
>
> — PABLO PICASSO

CARMEN IS A BACKYARD ARTIST. She's ten years old, and she loves to be outdoors. She gathers treasures—rocks, flowers (a.k.a. dandelions), sticks, anything that catches her fancy—and creates neatly arranged monuments with them. Sometimes she displays them on the platform of her wooden swing set; other times, they'll be in the middle of the yard—at least until her dad's lawnmower finds them.

As Carmen has gotten older, her time in the backyard has dwindled. Now, she spends more of her time in front of textbooks.

"She hasn't gotten to the point where she doesn't want to go to school—yet," her father, John, a technology integration specialist in central Indiana told us. "But when she comes home and I ask, 'Hey, how was school today?' she'll say, 'Oh, I've got so much homework to do.' She never talks anymore about what was fun or what the best part of her day was. Now, homework is a constant struggle."

Sometimes John will pull Carmen away from her homework so she can just be a kid. They'll go outdoors, and she'll chatter and play again like when she was younger. "I can almost see her brain working when she's outside. That's what I miss. That's what I'm afraid she's going to be missing," John said, "because I can't see her brain working when she's trying to define an answer from the text".

Homework Is a Contentious Topic

Everyone—from educators to students to business people to politicians—seems to have an opinion on homework. It's a hot topic! And people get riled up easily about it.

Students generally dislike homework because they're the ones doing it. And who can blame them? Often, homework consists of uninspiring exercises, busywork, or repetitive problems. Students often see homework as drudgery—a hoop they have to jump through en route to free time that they can spend the way they want.

Teachers are a mixed bag when it comes to homework. Some see it as a rite of passage—as educational lore they must perpetuate. Others believe homework is effective because they have seen student achievement rise when it has been assigned. Still others are frustrated, recognizing that the convention of homework is twisted and imperfect, but they don't know what to do about it.

Parents are the ones pulled in the most directions by homework. They remember being plagued by it during their own childhood. They have a front-row seat to their children's rolling eyes, frustrated outbursts, or defeated sobs over assignments. Parents fight and fight and fight with their kids about whether homework is finished, whether it's done well, and whether there's more they're hiding. But parents also want the best for their children. Some hope that, if teachers throw enough homework at their children, the information will stick and they will become exceptional adults.

"When I was in the fourth grade, my teacher was famous for giving hours of daily homework. I remember working all afternoon and then crying because I still wasn't finished and couldn't watch TV with my family. Much more than what I learned via the homework assignment, I remember being extremely frustrated and feeling very sad to miss my favorite show."

—Karen Mensing, first and second grade teacher

Administrators face multiple issues when it comes to homework. On one hand, they see the research indicating that homework is not effective. On the other hand, principals, superintendents, and other school leaders are responsible to the community and the government if test scores don't measure up. Administrators know that the public may label their schools as "too soft" or "not rigorous enough" if homework isn't assigned to students.

Business people see education through the lens of the college graduates they employ. It's easy for them to support homework—and more of it! They simply want better educated employees.

Then there are politicians. Let's not even go there.

As you can see, coming to a general consensus about homework is as tricky as deciding between the Salisbury steak and the chicken patty in the cafeteria. (They might actually be the same thing, you know.)

WHAT IS HOMEWORK?

What is homework anyway? The word implies that it is work students do at home. However, homework is a concept, not a specific activity or object.

Things we send home that some people consider homework include:

- Papers requiring parent signatures
- Studying
- Independent practice
- Research papers
- Worksheets
- Book work
- Project work
- Viewing videos
- Group collaboration
- Independent reading
- Busywork
- Flashcards
- Boxes of Kleenex to school for extra credit

Is homework always a learning activity? Not necessarily.

For the purposes of this book, we're defining *homework* as any academic work done outside of class: at home, before or after school, in the hall before class, or even during another teacher's class. (Yes, we admit it happens!)

So *homework* consists of any assigned task slated to be done outside the hours of class. What the word *homework* does not describe is the quality or quantity of the task, a reality that makes homework discussions challenging because it turns into a war of vocabulary. For example, if two people discuss their children's homework, one could be railing against mindless worksheets while the other is in favor of carefully crafted activities prompting students to reflect or create. But instead of naming the specific activity, they both refer to the tasks simply as "homework." And so one parent wonders why on earth anyone would be a proponent of (mindless) homework while the other can't understand why a parent *wouldn't* want their child to do (relevant and creative) work at home. Neither parent understands the other's point of view because they aren't speaking the same language about homework.

Why Do Teachers Give Homework?

When I (Alice) first started teaching, I assumed I should assign homework. I was given homework as a student, so I never even considered *not* assigning homework. Truthfully, I gave very little thought to whether homework was really necessary or helpful; it was just part of my lesson. My daily practice was to end the lesson and assign problems from the book. In fact, this habit was so routine that I had sections of my whiteboard reserved for classwork (CW) and homework (HW). I simply filled in the assignments on the board each morning.

Early on, I gave my students a packet of worksheets to do during every single break. Why? Because I assumed that is what teachers were supposed to do. Then before one break, I was behind on my work and didn't get around to making the packet. To my amazement, the sky did not fall. Better yet, my students actually got to enjoy their break. Or rather, I should say they got to enjoy the night before the end of break. Teachers who assign homework during school breaks always assume (hope!) that their students will do a worksheet or two a day to keep the material fresh in their minds. Yeah, right. The more common practice is for students to spend their vacation time doing what they want while quietly dreading the looming homework assignment. Then, they cram in the worksheets, writing assignment, or art project at the last second.

I'm a math teacher, so I ran some correlational numbers comparing student grades and test scores to homework completion. Sure enough, the students who did the homework performed better on the test. However, those students were more advanced in the first place. I realized the students who did the homework weren't the ones who needed it. So I stopped assigning homework.

Yes, you read that correctly. I teach high school math, and I stopped assigning homework. And guess what? Test scores did *not* go down. Even better, my students' enjoyment of math went up.

If you're like I was, homework might be a given. A habit. You probably spent hours doing homework for your classes as a student, and you may assume that it is necessary. But in this book, we're asking you to challenge that assumption. If you are wondering if it's even possible to ditch that homework, here are a few questions to consider before giving homework for your next lesson:

Does it increase a student's love of learning?

Does it *significantly* increase learning?

Does it stimulate students' interest in the subject and make them want to delve deeper?

Are students able to complete the assignment without help?

Is it differentiated for ability or interest?

If the students didn't have to do it, would they *want* to do it anyway?

Is it fair to all students, especially those from poorer families and less-educated households?

Does it avoid causing fights, parent/child division, and a lack of harmony in the home?

If you answer "no" to these questions, maybe it's time to ditch that homework and try something else instead.

Ditch That Homework Resources

No teacher believes he is assigning busywork, yet many students and parents feel inundated by it. Determining whether something is actually busywork or an important element of the learning process can be complicated.

We have created a survey to help you evaluate your assignments. While nothing specifically makes a task busywork, the higher the score on the survey, the more likely the assignment may be busywork.

Busywork survey: DitchThatHomework.com/busywork

Why Is Homework a Bad Idea?

All of our results indicate that homework as it is now being assigned discriminates against children whose parents don't have a college degree, against parents who have English as a second language, against, essentially, parents who are poor (Wallace 2015).

Academic benefits are not the only consideration in the homework debate. Ideally, education should "level the playing field," but homework has the potential to create inequitable learning environments. Access to resources is unequal: parental support and tutoring, high-speed Internet, quiet work spaces, and role models may not be available or, if they are, may need to be shared among several siblings.

"My kids also participated in sports and/or band. The school put so much pressure on them to get involved in these things. But it made for twelve-hour (or longer) school days. Adding the homework load on top of that meant my kids got less than six hours of sleep a night during the week, and they developed serious health issues. I felt powerless to fight this battle for my kids. Neglecting homework wasn't an option, as this would have led to lower grades and they couldn't have participated in the extracurricular activities. Looking back, the only worthwhile assignment my four kids did during high school was a senior budgeting project where they learned some real-life lessons. The rest simply robbed us of family time and my kids' last years of childhood."

—CHERYL OGLE, PARENT

In addition to the challenges some students may face in regard to resources, time (or lack thereof) is a serious issue. Family situations today are complicated. In nearly half of all two-parent families, both parents work (Miller 2015). That means time as a family can be very limited, and homework puts a burden on organizing it. It is stressful (sometimes impossible) for my husband and me (Alice) to police my kids' homework. Mornings are a frenzy, highlighted by trying to make lunches without any bread—not what I would describe as "quality" family time. After school, we are our kids' personal Uber drivers, chauffeuring them from school to activities. Evenings are spent scraping together dinner. Down times are few and far between and, personally, I don't want to waste those precious moments on third-grade math homework.

"Homework often requires parent assistance, which is unfair. Homework is independent practice—not a second job for parents."

—JACK JARVIS, RETIRED TEACHER AND PARENT

More than once, I have been over at a friend's house for dinner and my friend's child *didn't have time* to join us for dinner due to homework. Never have I heard, "But this assignment is super valuable, so I'm glad my child is doing it." Almost always, the parent laments that homework disrupts their ability to make family plans. It is difficult, perhaps impossible, to pinpoint the impact homework assignments have on a family.

"I already don't give homework for a variety of reasons, but mostly because it became a greater separator of the haves and have nots. I was giving grades based on socioeconomics, which is classist and against my beliefs as an educator. I think the turning point for me was when I had a kid working third shift at the chicken plant from 11:00 p.m. to 7:00 a.m. and then coming to school until 4:00 p.m.—to then go home and get some sleep before he went back to work. So I practice as much as I can during the class period."

—KASEY NORED, TEACHER

Our Beef with Homework

People argue convincingly on both sides of the homework debate. In fact, piles of research have been published to support both arguments. Practically everyone, including teachers, administrators, parents, and students, has formed strong opinions based on a mix of theory, research, and life experience.

We (Alice and Matt) fall into the "no homework" camp. (That's probably obvious from the title of the book, right?) We intend for *Ditch That Homework* to be a handbook and treasure trove of strategies and ideas for becoming less reliant on homework. Before we get into the *how* of ditching homework, we want to give you our *why* for writing this book—the reasons we believe teachers should ditch that homework.

- **Research is unclear on the benefits of homework**. Alfie Kohn, who has studied, researched, and written extensively about homework, has reviewed numerous studies on homework. In his book, *The Homework Myth*, he states his conclusion:

  > *Taken as a whole, the available research might be summarized as inconclusive. But if we look more closely, even that description turns out to be too generous ... Careful examination of the data raises serious doubts about whether meaningful learning is enhanced by homework for most students (Kohn 2006).*

- **Kids often just won't do homework**. You can reward them, cajole them, threaten or harass them. You can even warn them that poor grades will affect their college entrance or their ability to get a job. Still, some students just won't do

WHY DITCH HOMEWORK?

(1) EQUITY FOR ALL STUDENTS =

Home situations, resources, and parent time are not equal. Not all kids get the same level of support at home.

(2) STRESS & FAMILY FIGHTING

Homework is a known source of stress and fighting for families. Homework adds to it.

(3) SMALL ACADEMIC BENEFITS

Research shows the level of academic benefit to be negligible. It's not a good investment of time.

(4) CHEATING

The truth: students copy assignments. Some parents have been known to do work for their kids.

(5) DIFFICULT TO DIFFERENTIATE

Students have different interest levels and abilities. One may need extra practice that another doesn't.

(6) REDUCES LOVE OF LEARNING

Motivation is key. Students are either curious and want to learn, or they're reluctant and forced to do it.

Icons: Kevin, Karthik Srinivas, Gan Khoon Lay, Severino Ribecca, Arjun Mahanti via The Noun Project

DITCH THAT HOMEWORK

homework—especially if they feel it's meaningless. Others will do the homework, but only halfheartedly, perhaps hurriedly in the hallway before school, or in another teacher's class.

- **Homework can have negative effects on students' bodies.** Research shows more homework can lead to less sleep for kids, which can cause obesity and attention deficit hyperactivity disorder (ADHD) (Galloway, Conner & Pope 2013). The severe stress associated with meeting expectations related to homework, struggling with assignments, and arguing with parents about them can be just as damaging.

- **Homework can smother a child's love of learning.** Children are naturally curious. They're learning all the time, whether they realize it or not. Humans are hardwired to learn. But when learning is forced and inauthentic, it becomes a taskmaster instead of a muse. When the fairy dust of learning disappears, it is hard to get the magic back.

RESEARCH JUST CONFUSES THE ISSUE

Parents, administrators, teachers—everyone with a stake in the homework debate—wants to know what the research says. Hundreds of academic studies have measured homework and its impact. The studies show mixed results on whether homework is effective. Aside from the conflicting findings, one of the chief problems with these studies is that most of them measure the efficacy of homework based on students' ability to improve their test scores.

Students are more than the sum of their test scores! I (Matt) want my kids to be fantastic human beings when they grow up. I want them to be kind, compassionate, and generous. I want them to be curious and passionate about something. Sure, I want them to be intelligent and informed, too, but knowledge is just one part of a bigger picture. When research reduces kids to test scores, it dehumanizes them into a one-dimensional stream of numbers.

The problem is, most homework research shows correlation rather than causation. When two numbers correlate, a relationship exists between them; they're connected in some way. But correlation doesn't equal causation. Causation is a much higher standard: It says one thing *caused* another thing.

If a homework study suggests that homework is correlated with higher test scores, we need to understand what that really means. Making a correlational connection between homework and test scores oversimplifies the situation. Many variables are at play here—household income, compliance, parental involvement, cheating, and more—which means it is difficult to isolate the connection specifically between homework and test scores.

Here's an example: Harris Cooper, a Duke University professor and expert in the field of homework, wrote in a well-publicized 1989 research analysis, "There is no evidence that any amount of homework improves the academic performance of elementary students." In the same study, he reports that homework improves academic achievement more in grades seven through nine and even more in grades ten through twelve. But what is homework here, exactly? And is academic achievement—points in a gradebook—the true definition of success?

One deficiency in most research on homework is its vague definition of "homework." It lumps word searches and mindless multiple-choice worksheets in with the kind of assignments that really cause kids to think, discuss, and create. Not all assignments are created equal. Unfortunately, most homework research does nothing to separate poorly designed busywork from quality academic work.

When research has such a narrow view of students and the kind of work they do, the light it can shed on the topic of homework is limited. And sadly, the research never asks the important question: Is homework necessary?

At What Cost?

We (Matt and Alice) do all-day professional development sessions with teachers. We introduce new ideas, answer questions, demonstrate, and give teachers time to work. It is not uncommon for teachers to be totally spent by the end of our workshops. Their eyes and body language offer clear indication when they are maxed out on learning. At some point in these seven-hour sessions, it becomes obvious that asking them to do anything else or trying to cram anything else into their brains is futile.

> All their work is done in class, in front of me. I know they did it and not someone else (not copied it from a friend); and if they have questions, I am there to help (unlike if they go home to an empty house). We have 70-minute classes, and I allow time for work to be done in class. Students would rather work than listen to my coffee-fueled sermons anyway. Demonstrate, then let them apply the knowledge. If they finish early and correctly, I let them play games. Yes, you read that right. Why not? They did what they were supposed to do, so they get rewarded."
>
> —ROBIN PERRY, HIGH SCHOOL BUSINESS EDUCATION TEACHER

Seven hours is a long time to exercise your brain and learn new things. While most teachers are excited about learning ideas to improve their classes, after seven hours of work, I (Alice) suspect their excitement would disappear if they were assigned two more hours of work to do at home.

But that is exactly what kids are asked to do every day. And it has costs.

Teachers send home worksheets with students after a full day of school work and ask them to do problems one through thirty (odd numbers only). The kids see little benefit and, after a long day, the repetitive practice isn't very stimulating, so they put forth only the bare minimum effort required to complete it. Their brains aren't engaged, so very little (if any) learning happens. In her 2015 book, *Mathematical Mindsets*, Stanford researcher Jo Boaler even goes so far as to say that "there is a lot of evidence that homework, of any form, is unnecessary and damaging."

Sure, they've invested some time in the activity, but what did they get in return for their investment? Hours of extra work, frustration, and reinforcement of mistakes (because practice makes permanent, you know, even when they're practicing errors). What they *don't* get is the kind of excitement or wonder that makes them want to be independent, lifelong learners. In short, students see little to no return on their investment.

We *must* do better.

How Should We Proceed?

Our lives get busier every year. Family time and time for self-direction, though critical to our well-being, are in short supply. On the upside, we have access to technology, best practices, research, scientific findings, and ideas that can make us—both educators and students—more productive and more efficient.

Our students face a future where problem-solving, teamwork, communication, and creativity will be rewarded. Homework that requires superficial thinking or rote busywork does not equip students for that future. It's no wonder that they shirk, procrastinate, or cheat to get their homework done.

The question we all ask is this: If research on homework is confusing and inconclusive and opinions on the topic are so divergent, why is homework still the status quo in schools—especially when there's no proof that it's effective?

Something doesn't add up. Clearly, it's time to change the status quo.

It's time to *Ditch That Homework*.

The premise of this book is simple: to render homework obsolete. Imagine what would happen if you made your classes more efficient and effective, progressively lessening the need for homework. What would your class, your day, your students' days look like if you ditched your homework entirely? As you read on, you'll discover how the relationships and learning in your classroom can improve when the focus isn't on homework. You'll also get a glimpse of what those after-school hours could look like for you and your students. Wouldn't it be nice *not* to spend hours grading homework each night? We think so. We also love the idea of kids having time to pursue *their* interests at home, even if that simply means playing outside with friends.

Here are just a few ways to stop relying on homework:

- Design for more active student engagement during class time.

- Allow students to choose routes and topics for learning and meeting educational goals while touching on their personal interests.

- Show your students that you know, respect, and care for them so that they *want* to take up your mission as their own.

- Use technology to work smarter, more efficiently, effectively, and creatively.

- Implement scientifically proven learning methods that optimize the way the brain works.

- Empower your students to think for themselves and guide them to becoming lifelong learners.

When you employ modern teaching techniques to optimize learning to its peak in the classroom, it becomes possible to accomplish all that you need to during the school day, which makes homework less and less of a necessity.

Until, one day, you are able to ditch it. Completely.

Ultimately, the choice is yours. Is homework the best fit for your students? As we said, our goal is to provide you with strategies, ideas, philosophies, and stories from real teachers to empower you to *Ditch That Homework*. Ultimately, we hope that you (and your students' families) will be able to enjoy more family time, experience better health, and rediscover a pure love of learning.

Let's get started.

WHAT DO WE DO INSTEAD?

CHAPTER 1
DITCH THAT TEXTBOOK

> USING TECHNOLOGY TO
> REMIX "TEXTBOOK"
> ACTIVITIES AND PRACTICES

TEXTBOOKS WERE AMONG THE FIRST WIRE-LESS LEARNING DEVICES — EDUCATION WE COULD TAKE ON THE GO. They were often the focal point for education at many levels and served an important purpose for a long time, but times have changed. So have our wireless devices.

Textbooks today are symbols of the past, a time when the modus operandi was marching chapter by chapter through a textbook and answering questions at the end. But today, we have access to so many resources. The most important of those resources isn't an app or a digital tool. It's the brain of a well-trained educator, who can design educational tasks that stimulate, inspire, and equip students.

I (Matt) talk to educators all over the United States about ditching textbooks. Many of them assume I'm going to tell them that textbooks are evil and that they should deposit them in the nearest dumpster with a resounding thud. Not true. Textbooks are a resource, a tool; I'm not about to suggest widespread removal of them from the hands of teachers and students. But textbooks are just one of the many tools at our disposal.

Today's technology gives us, as educators, the ability to connect to people, places, and ideas worldwide—in real time! Rather than relying blindly on a textbook that was created by a company that doesn't know our students and their needs, we can create and share and remix and innovate every lesson we teach. That means we have the potential to educate students in more powerful and meaningful ways than ever before.

When you use your creative, innovative capacities to deliver stimulating and engaging lessons, you tend to use textbooks less. And the less you use textbooks, the more likely it is that you'll find that you don't need to rely on homework to reinforce concepts because the learning that happens in the classroom *sticks*. We've seen it happen time after time. Teachers stop depending on textbooks. They start creating more relevant and creative lessons. Students become more focused, attentive, and engaged in learning because they are actually interested in learning; it's something they *want* to do. That kind of hyper-attentiveness locks in learning.

So how do you do that? How can you ditch outdated, ineffective "textbook" practices in your classroom in favor of something fresh and new, something that will also help you ditch homework in the process?

Here are a few ideas that have worked for us.

Ditch Those Worksheets

In the first few years of my teaching career, I (Matt) relied on my textbooks and *lots* of corresponding worksheets. Creating my own worksheets kind of excited me. But after those first few years of worksheets, workbooks, and end-of-chapter questions, I came to a scary realization: My high school Spanish students couldn't speak Spanish. Plus, they were so bored with my lessons I wasn't connecting with them. Neither was my content.

Something had to change. I realized I had to break myself of my worksheet habit. Rather than helping my students practice their language skills, all those worksheets had become were drill-and-kill tools of boredom, frustration, and shallow learning. Thankfully, breaking that habit didn't require much—if any—extra effort. If you are ready to break your own worksheet habit, here are few things to try:

1. **Use manipulatives instead.** Cut-out sheets of paper, blocks, or any other object that students can touch and engage the brain in different ways more than a sheet of paper does. Manipulatives help students of all ages wrap their brains around new ideas.

2. **Go deep with one question.** Many worksheets repeat the same activity over and over and over (*e.g.*, addition problems, verb conjugation, etc.). Asking students to think through one higher-level question and provide a deeper explanation of the answer or concept may be more worthwhile than asking lots of lower-level questions.

3. **Draw a picture.** Making concepts visual is powerful because the human brain processes pictures differently than words. The brain doesn't work in words; it translates them into pictures when we think. We may communicate our ideas in words, but our brain doesn't use them. Drawing a simple picture on a piece

of paper lets students *see* the idea instead of simply envisioning it. (And envisioning an abstract concept can be harder for students than teachers think it should be!) You're not limited to paper, either. Shaving cream on a desktop works well, too!

4. **Screencast videos.** Having students record audio and video of themselves explaining a new concept may not take any longer than filling in blanks on a worksheet, but the activity is much more engaging. Doing activities like screencast videos taps into students' creative capacities. If they've created it and are going to show it to their peers, students have more incentive to do their best work. Tools like Screencast-O-Matic (screencast-o-matic.com) and Educreations (iTunes: free) get students recording in no time.

5. **Shoot a quick video.** Record a video using a smartphone, tablet, or use the upload button on YouTube with your laptop or Chromebook. Use a tool like Flipgrid (flipgrid.com) to ask students a question or prompt that they can answer with a quick video. You can make a talking head video or something more elaborate, like a skit or a news program. Just as with the screencast video, this hands-on activity gets students creating with content instead of just repeating it. Plus, many students have access to smartphones in order to create.

6. **Create a digital game like Kahoot! or Quizizz.** If you want to ask lots of questions and see how students perform, use a game-show style website to do the same thing in a much more engaging format. With both Kahoot! (kahoot.com) and Quizizz (quizizz.com), you can write your own questions and choose the correct answers. The site does the grading for you! Plus, both sites let you view and download results for each question by individual student. For a different twist, challenge

students to write the questions instead of just answering them. In Chapter 8, I'll show you how to eliminate worksheet homework with Quizizz.

7. **Stop the video and talk.** Asking students to "do this worksheet while/after watching a video" is a common, ineffective practice. Processing a video can be cognitively taxing for students, especially when the words or ideas are brand new to them. Likewise, writing down answers on a worksheet while watching a video can cause them to miss important concepts. Instead of showing comprehension of a video with a worksheet, stop the video to reinforce, explain, or reflect on the material. Another strategy is to use EDpuzzle (edpuzzle.com), which automatically stops a video periodically to ask students questions.

8. **Encourage independent research on the web.** Let students then do some simple search engine digging to find additional facts related to the topic you're teaching. Instead of giving them new information in class or in a chapter of the textbook, let them do the work! If a student's research turns up dubious information, don't scrap the entire activity. Rather, use the opportunity for a teaching moment. Review the site(s) where the student found the information and discuss what makes a credible, reliable source on the web.

9. **Mass produce questions.** Instead of answering questions on a worksheet, have students create questions themselves. The Right Question Institute (rightquestion.org) offers resources for teachers on Question Formulation Technique (QFT), a framework for helping students generate quality questions. Their steps include finding a question focus, following specific rules for generating questions, producing and categorizing questions, prioritizing them, finding next steps, and reflecting. Free

QFT resources can be found at rightquestion.org/educators/resources.

10. **Include a C.** An easy way to improve the Depth of Knowledge in an activity and to make it more relevant for students' lives and futures is to add one of the four Cs. Take a worksheet activity and infuse creativity, critical thinking, collaboration, and/or communication.

> "Ultimately, the projects, regardless of how long they were, proved to be more effective than homework because they were relevant and interesting."
>
> —PAUL DIETRICH, TEACHER

DITCH THOSE RESEARCH REPORTS

In high school and college, I (Matt) suffered through numerous research projects. I gathered data, cited sources, followed MLA style, and double spaced page after page. I turned in my work and collected a grade but, aside from one political science paper I keep in a trunk full of papers in my basement, I never did anything else with all those papers.

When students create research reports and papers, they ...

- Gather information
- Evaluate sources
- Organize and synthesize data
- Form ideas and cohesive thoughts

- Create a polished, finished product
- Cite where they got their information

Clearly, there are merits to doing research and writing reports or papers. The problem is that the finished product isn't relevant to the real world—in the workforce or in people's personal lives. Reports and papers often end up where mine always did—in the trash. If students are doing their best work to learn and create, shouldn't the final product be in a format they can be proud of—and that they want to show others?

It's time to turn research reports and papers into something meaningful. Try these alternatives:

1. **Websites**. By creating a free website using tools like Weebly and Google Sites, students are much more likely to attract others' attention to their work. Websites can be shared easily. They live on the web indefinitely where people can stumble upon them through Google searches. They can be updated, changed, or improved immediately. When students publish their work to a website, they create a positive digital footprint, and if they add content year by year, the site becomes a digital portfolio.

2. **Infographics**. You've probably seen super-long infographics on Pinterest and other social media sites. You have to scroll down through to see all the information, and you keep scrolling because, why not? They're interesting and easy to read. Here are two great tools your students can use to create their own infographics:

   - *Piktochart* (piktochart.com) can turn a report or paper into a flashy, eye-catching visual. Students can start with a predesigned template or use the graphics, text, and other goodies to create their own infographics from scratch.

- *Canva's* (canva.com) drag-and-drop interface lets students create beautiful designs. They can start with a perfectly sized infographic template, add the text and visuals they want, then save them as image files for the web or in PDF format for sharing and printing.

3. **Google Drawings interactive posters.** Displaying lots of information from a research project on a poster board might be impossible—or require teeny-tiny text! A Google Drawings interactive poster is great for an in-depth research project because it can be a jumping off point for more information. Students can use Google Drawings to present visuals in a digital poster format that includes links to Google Docs or other resources to provide more information about their topic.

DITCH THAT HOMEWORK RESOURCES

When creating interactive posters, use these tips:

Be sure to use a live hyperlink (Ctrl+K is the keyboard shortcut) to get readers where they want to go.

Use links to pull in multimedia. Send readers to a video, an interactive slideshow, or an audio file you've found on the web that adds value to the project.

Add images responsibly. Include images with a Creative Commons license (search.creativecommons.org) or from the public domain. Cite those images appropriately. Students will learn a lot about respecting others' intellectual property through this process.

Interactive posters:
DitchThatHomework.com/interactiveposters

---

4. **YouTube playlists.** Researchers gather information and present it in video format to an audience of millions every day. *It's called television news.* Students can do the same thing by creating short videos on the different segments of their research project. (See No. 5 in the *Ditch Those Worksheets* section above.) Then, they can upload the videos to YouTube and link them together with a playlist. The end product is an interactive video version of their research, their own version of "newscasting."

5. **Radio shows.** Programs like *This American Life* and other audio documentaries do a phenomenal job of creating long-form stories and journalistic presentations in an engaging way. With some planning, students could record a compelling podcast or radio show presentation about their content. They could add interviews, sound effects, background audio from a site like a restaurant or a bus station, etc. Using tools like Screencastify to record and Audacity or GarageBand to mix the audio, students can make shows that are as simple or complex as they dare to make them.

6. **Info/image slideshow.** The *Did You Know?/Shift Happens* videos, created by Karl Fisch and Scott McLeod, have been viewed millions of times on YouTube. These engaging videos teach viewers about rapid changes that are happening globally. Students can create similar text-based slideshow videos using YouTube's photo slideshow tool or Animoto (free for educators).

7. **Blogs.** Knowing that an authentic audience (not "just" the teacher) will be reading or viewing their work is an incentive for students to put forth their very best effort. Blogs are the perfect option if you want to give students an authentic

audience that's potentially huge. Blogs differ from websites (see No. 1 above) in that they are well suited for publishing posts periodically over time. In contrast, a website is a better fit for a single project. Students can publish their work to a blog, and others from the school community—or around the world—can see it, leave comments, and discuss their work. (Most blogging platforms let teachers moderate comments before students see them.) Two popular platforms for student blogging include Blogger (*blogger.com*), which is free, and Edublogs (*edublogs. org*), which offers free and paid options.

Ditch Those Walls

Have you ever taken a trip that changed your worldview or made learning come alive? For me (Matt), it was a mission trip to Uruguay.

As an aspiring Spanish teacher, I had studied South American culture and the language. I had seen pictures and read vignettes about the people and their customs. But none of it really hit home until I set foot in Montevideo, Uruguay. I drank *yerba mate*, a green tea Uruguayans enjoy in social settings. I visited Colonia del Sacramento, a historic colonial town that runs alongside the Rio de la Plata River. I walked the small town's cobblestone streets and gazed up at its lighthouse. I tasted the local fare, including a *parrillada*, a variety of grilled meats that included blood sausage (a cultural experience that I'll never try again!).

South America wouldn't hold the special place in my heart it does now had I not seen and experienced it in such a personal way.

SEE THE WORLD VIRTUALLY

Traveling to new places can offer life-altering experiences, but it can also be expensive, time-consuming, and planning-intensive. Thankfully, students today don't have to leave the classroom to experience distant locales for themselves. With technology you already have, an Internet connection, and the courage to try something new, you can break down the walls of your classroom and empower your students to experience, communicate with, and learn from the world around them. Tools like Skype, Google Hangouts, and FaceTime give you and your students the ability to communicate face-to-face with people practically anywhere in the world. Using tools such as Google Docs, TodaysMeet, Voxer, and Padlet, your students can work on projects in real time with others worldwide. Here are a few ways to ditch those walls and expand your students' horizons (and we'll dive into how to make them happen momentarily):

- **Connect your classes to classes in other cities, states, and countries.** Share learning with other teachers and students, discuss topics of shared importance, and even collaborate on projects across the miles.

- **Invite guest speakers to your classes virtually.** Experts in your subject area can visit with students via Skype, Google Hangouts, or FaceTime to share their unique experiences, perspectives, and work. The two-way capabilities of this technology mean that students can ask questions face-to-face and talk with some of the top minds in the world.

- **Take students on virtual field trips to important landmarks, museums, parks, and other special sites.** Virtual tour guides can show students around their facilities, do demonstrations, and display artifacts for students to see.

EXAMPLES FROM THE CLASSROOM

Iowa fifth-grade teacher Gina Ruffcorn used video calls to make research and debate come alive for her students. While studying the topic of the treatment of animals, she coordinated a video call with the Ringling Bros. and Barnum & Bailey Center for Elephant Conservation in central Florida. Her students learned that the center is like a retirement home for elephants who have performed or been on exhibit in zoos their whole lives. They also heard from a representative of LionAid, a charity in the United Kingdom dedicated to saving all lions, who shared another side of the debate about the treatment of animals in captivity. The LionAid worker bluntly told students that lions lose their very essence of being lions when they're kept in captivity—in part because they can't hunt. After hearing from people on both sides of the animal captivity issue, the students had their own candid discussions related to humanity's effect on the environment. For Gina, the experiences she created during the unit were as much about meeting academic standards as they were about getting her students to really think about the issue. "I don't think my kids understand that, eventually, their generation is going to be in control of some of the legislation that will protect our environment,"

Gina said. "If I don't get them in touch with it in their younger years, how will they develop this awareness?" Before the unit was over, the students wrote letters petitioning the British prime minister (at the request of the LionAid worker) for cessation of wild game hunting.

Todd Shriver, an Indiana high school social studies teacher, offers an elective class about the history of the 1980s. His challenge is to make this period of time—when the students' parents were children—real to the students. His solution is to let students talk to the luminaries of the decade. Shriver schedules virtual interviews with personalities such as MTV's VJ Alan Hunter, *The Cosby Show's* Malcolm-Jamal Warner, and Mike Eruzione, the captain of the "Miracle on Ice" Olympic hockey game in 1980. "These 'experts' are able to share their experiences that cannot be found in textbooks," Todd said. "Our social studies department has been fortunate to establish a partnership with these individuals to continue speaking with our students each year."

Mike Soskil, head teacher at a Pennsylvania elementary school, turned a fun singing activity into a life-changing project. As his students were preparing for a choir performance, Mike arranged for them to sing to kids at a school in Nairobi, Kenya, via a Skype call. During the call, Mike's kids learned the Kenyan students lived in the cholera-ravaged Kibera Slum. Wanting to help, Mike's students coordinated with other schools to raise more than $12,000 to buy water filters for the Kenyan school and for the Kenyan students' homes. Mike

flew to Kenya and presented the water filters to the community while his students at home watched through teary eyes on Skype. "I knew that, for the rest of their lives, they would seek out ways to use their learning to do good in the world because helping others made them feel so good," Mike said.

Mike Soskil's students in Pennsylvania raised more than $12,000 to support students (pictured above) at Cheery Children Education Centre in Nairobi, Kenya.

How to Create Virtual Experiences for Your Students

Interacting with people from different cultures and areas of expertise creates the kind of learning that sticks with students long-term—the kind of learning that doesn't need homework. Those encounters help students make a personal connection with the content and with people they're meeting. The emotion students feel in experiences like these builds long-term memory, notes Eric Jensen in his book *Superteaching*. The more intensely that you engage the emotions, the longer you'll recall what you have learned (Jensen 2008). Worksheets pale in comparison to the kind of learning that happens with intimate interaction. When it comes time to recall facts, relay experiences, or express opinions, the information learned during conversations from video calls will come flooding back to students.

Where can you find these classes, guests, and field trips? Several great resources include the Skype in the Classroom site *(SkypeInTheClassroom.com)* and Nepris *(nepris.com)*. Skype in the Classroom is an online database of classes, guests, and virtual field trip locations. Nepris *(nepris.com)* connects teachers and students with STEM/STEAM industry experts virtually, giving students valuable experiences and allowing companies to extend education outreach. Additionally, several Google Plus communities are dedicated to helping fellow educators create memorable Google Hangouts experiences in the classroom, including:

- Mystery Location Calls *(DitchThatHomework.com/mlc)*

- Google Hangouts in Education
  (DitchThatHomework.com/ghe)

- Mystery Hangout *(DitchThatHomework.com/mh)*

- Educators on Google Plus *(DitchThatHomework.com/egp)*

- Global Education Conference *(DitchThatHomework.com/gec)*

If you can't find what you're looking for there, just dream and then ask. Think of whom you'd really like to connect with, then send that person or company an email or message via social media. You might be surprised at who says *"yes"* to your request for a virtual interview. If your students are reading a book and the author is alive, send him or her an email invitation to video call your class. Children's book authors often love connecting with the kids who read their books and can talk about the subject matter as well as about writing and publishing.

TAKE THE FIRST STEP

Will rethinking worksheets and research papers eliminate the need for homework? Will video calls reinvent the way students learn? Maybe not in isolation or all at once. But these ideas are about how we've changed the way we teach and learn, little by little. We've found that by being intentional about the way new ideas are introduced in the classroom, it's possible to improve the way students process, use, and remember the material. In contrast, when we do the same old thing, day after day, we fall into a teaching rut. If you've been there, you know that those ruts are just as boring for your students as they are for you. Mentally, our students check out when their cognitive and creative abilities aren't engaged. By breaking out of traditional molds and ditching the textbook and routine mentality, you can help your students maintain razor-sharp focus on the ideas of the day.

And if that doesn't *reduce* the need to assign homework, nothing will.

CHAPTER 2
DITCH THAT LECTURE

> GETTING KIDS CONNECTED
> TO CONTENT AND LEARNING
> IN NEW WAYS

EARLY IN MY TEACHING CAREER, I (ALICE) SPENT SIGNIFICANT TIME DURING EVERY CLASS DOING HOMEWORK-RELATED STUFF. Going over the homework. Collecting the homework. Recording the homework. Having students call home about missing homework. None of those activities actively involved students in their learning.

The first five minutes of class are golden. It's the time teachers are most likely to have their students' attention. And how did I use those valuable minutes? By providing an engaging learning hook? By asking a thought-provoking question to kick-start thinking on the day's learning? Nope. We went over homework. Golden time *wasted*.

After all of that procedural work surrounding homework, I typically gave my students directions for the day. Picture it: Students passively waited for me to finish collecting homework. Then they sat and passively listened to me before getting their instructions.

Great way to energize a day of learning, huh?

After giving directions and finally saying "go," I almost always heard at least one student ask, "OK, what are we doing again?" It seemed as if my class ran on a loop: All of that work and effort at the beginning of every day with *very* little learning to show for it.

The reality is that, even when they are paying attention, students are not memorizing every word you say. They can't recall every detail of a lecture or all the directions for their classwork. And then, of course, there are always students who aren't even in the room (e.g., absent students or those who have been called out of class) to hear the lecture or directions. And forget about trying to differentiate for learning needs with spoken directions to the whole class. That just adds to the confusion.

Let's Get Kids Locked In to Learning

To stop relying on homework, we must change how our classrooms function day to day—from the moment the kids walk through the door. Moving away from a teacher-centered classroom to a more student-centered model is a great start. (Students shouldn't have to wait passively for teachers to tell them what to do.) Capturing students' attention by connecting learning to their unique interests is another vital move. (We are all more likely to remember what we learn if we're interested in the topic in the first place.)

Real learning—lasting learning—is the result of one word: engagement.

Engagement can be defined in a few ways:

- To occupy, attract, or involve (someone's interest or attention)
- To participate or become involved in
- To establish a meaningful contact or connection with
- To move into position so as to come into operation (like engaging a clutch in a car)

Real engagement conjures the idea of being completely locked in and actively connected.

When students are disengaged, they're not paying attention. When that happens, it doesn't matter how well we've fine-tuned our lesson plans. It doesn't matter how comprehensive the lecture is. It doesn't matter how rigorous the work is. The learning simply won't stick.

In contrast, if students are engaged—locked in—to what they're learning, the learning is more likely to stick. So how can you do that? How can you get your students to lock in on learning? Here are some ideas.

Make Directions and Information Accessible to Students

Posting lesson information and basic directions for tasks where it can be easily accessed and referred to by students allows the teacher to spend more time working one-on-one with students.

Use your classroom website, learning-management system, or Google Classroom to disseminate directions. Students walk in the classroom, go to the website, and get to work. Create a daily agenda and include directions for tasks in that digital space. Directions can be written or include visual, short videos or short animations. If it isn't possible to post this information in a digital format, create a physical space in your room where students can access your "get started" content as soon as they arrive each day. So that students can get to work as soon as they walk in the class, I (Alice) always make my first agenda item something they can do independently.

> "To reduce my dependency on homework, I am curating lots of online resources and tools for my students to use. I simply post the tools on Google Classroom and the students have access to them 24/7."
>
> —HEIDI TRUDE, TEACHER

DITCH THAT HOMEWORK RESOURCES

Placing directions on your classroom website also provides transparency. If parents can access it, they know what their child is doing each day. Students who are absent can complete their work from home. A website also makes it easier to collaborate and share with other teachers. Karly Moura, a teacher on special assignment (TOSA) from California, says that in some classes at her school, parents ask for homework even if the teachers don't give it. ("Yup, it happens!" she says.) A classroom website is a great place to post extra practice for struggling students or for those families who request it.

6 OPPORTUNITIES TO INCREASE CLASSROOM EFFICIENCY

(1) GET STARTED RIGHT AWAY

What are students doing the minute they walk in the door? Plan for a student activity.

(2) STOP GIVING DIRECTIONS

How do students figure out what they should be doing besides waiting to be told?

(3) LOOK UP INFORMATION

What can students look up instead of copying down? Include search questions in the lesson.

(4) CROWDSOURCE

Have students share what they find. Divide and conquer!

(5) USE DIGITAL FEEDBACK

What can students get immediate digital feedback on rather than waiting for it to be graded or going over it?

(6) CHANGE CONVERSATIONS

Use your words to encourage students and increase critical thinking.

Icons: Garrett Knoll, Gregor Cresnar, Davo Sime, dilayorganci, Loudoun Design Co. via The Noun Project

DITCH THAT HOMEWORK

Some teachers have shared their concerns with us about student-directed classrooms. They wonder if they will be viewed negatively for not doing their jobs if they let technology deliver the directions or if they allow students to use the Internet or apps to find answers. Some even worry that technology will replace them as teachers.

To those conscientious teachers we say this: Relax. Computers and technology do not reduce the importance of the teacher. In fact, the exact opposite is true!

Yes, if your sole responsibility in the classroom was to deliver information, you could be replaced by YouTube and Google. But your role is about so much more than lectures and instructions.

Today's technology allows teachers to reduce time spent disseminating information and directions. It gives us more time to work with students on building critical-thinking skills. It allows us to engage in interesting projects and discussions with students and to provide high-quality feedback. Instead of replacing teachers, technology empowers us, as educators, to do what we do best—and what helps our students the most.

Focus on the Student, Not the Teacher

An important shift can happen the moment we start planning the day's lesson. Instead of focusing on what you, the teacher, are doing during a lesson, try to word your lesson plans so that you are planning what the students are doing. It's tough, but try to avoid saying "I" or "Teacher is" when planning out the lesson steps. Obviously you are doing things, but what lens do you write your lesson plan through— that of the teacher or that of the student? Instead, what if you gave them a juicy essential question, something that makes students say, "I want to learn that!"? A favorite example comes from Robert Kaplinsky's blog (robertkaplinsky.com). His juicy essential question: How can we #SaveNelly? (See more at DitchThatHomework.com/savenelly.) The rapper famously got behind on paying his taxes and his fans tried to help him recover by streaming his songs to earn him money. It's a great practice in multiplying and dividing decimals. What student wouldn't want to use math class to figure out how to save a famous rapper?

RETHINK INDEPENDENT PRACTICE

Most lesson plan templates mention "independent practice" and for good reason. It offers students the chance to put into practice what they've learned. It's a true test of the students' skills. Independent practice is essential. Many times, though, teachers assume independent practice means *homework*. If students take independent practice work home, what happens when they get stuck, make a mistake, or are unclear about the directions? No matter how clear I thought I made my directions, some students always had questions. Everyone filters information differently. Everyone has different life experiences that color their unique interpretations. As a teacher, I want to be there to support my students as they do independent practice and to clarify directions. This means they need to do the work in class.

Doing independent practice in the classroom lets students access a great resource: their highly skilled teacher. Students see teachers every day for good reason: We're trained in pedagogy, learning theory, and best practices. We're experts in our content area, and we have experience in helping learners succeed. Why would we want to disconnect students from this valuable resource?

DITCH THAT HOMEWORK RESOURCES

Certain elements of a lesson really make it catch on with students. A juicy essential question, the four Cs, and student exploration are a few things that help learning stick. We've developed a lesson plan template that walks you through some of the essential parts of creating an engaging lesson plan. You can make your own copy of the lesson plan template into your Google Drive or just use the prompts to guide your planning.

Lesson plan template:
DitchThatHomework.com/lessonplan

When we send work home with students, we put parents in the position of trying to be that highly skilled teacher. That's not fair to them. Nor is it fair to students whose parents aren't equipped to help with topics they were not trained on.

Students can and should do independent practice in the presence of their highly skilled teacher. When the classroom is student-centered, teachers are free to provide the support that students crave.

> DOING INDEPENDENT PRACTICE IN THE CLASSROOM LETS STUDENTS ACCESS A GREAT RESOURCE: THEIR HIGHLY SKILLED TEACHER.

"I taught high school math, and many of those kids had NO ONE to ask about homework if they took it home, so I made them do it in class with me."

—ROBIN PERRY, HIGH SCHOOL BUSINESS EDUCATION TEACHER

"I haven't given homework in over seven years. I feel it is a waste of the students' time, as well as my own! I teach seventh grade science. I do not focus on facts but on application of skills. We use our class time to learn (I rarely lecture) and the students complete their assignments in class."

—KELLY HEBERT, MIDDLE SCHOOL SCIENCE TEACHER

"More often than not, we both get frustrated because the homework makes no sense. Or we argue about how to solve the math problem because I'm not doing it correctly. More often than not, it's pages of worksheets that are not teaching them anything except to skim and find the answer."

—KATY HABIB, PARENT

"Ultimately, it means a change in approach at the classroom level. Students need lots of practice if teachers do all the work in class."

—JOE CARUSO, SECONDARY NUMERACY LEAD

ALICE'S DIGITAL FEEDBACK CYCLE

Here's how Alice makes the most of her class time with timely feedback.

---

(1) COLLABORATIVE DOC

Create a collaborative document that allows all the students in the class to work together. Tip: have students sitting in groups.

(2) FOCUS AND REDIRECT

Help students get on task. Are their devices charged? Do they need to put away something distracting?

(3) CONTRIBUTE/COMMENT

Students add ideas and information to the collaborative document and comment on peers' work.

(4) SIT NEXT TO A KID

Sit next to a student and provide feedback on his/her work. Then sit next to another student and provide feedback.

(5) MAKE DIGITAL COMMENTS

Do not sit down. Contribute two separate feedback comments to the collaborative document.

(6) REPEAT THE CYCLE

Continue this cycle until the allotted time for the activity is completed.

Icons: arjuazka, AlePio, iconsphere, Gerald Wildmoser, Gregor Cresnar via TheNounProject.com

DITCH THAT HOMEWORK

"It's practice, right? So I do more frequent checks—chunking by teaching one skill and giving them a chance to practice. I wander around and give feedback and ask questions. I review the next day by giving them a quick Socrative quiz of three-to-five questions over the material from the day before. It helps me to see immediately what they did not grasp and remember and helps me to reteach or fine-tune what I taught the day before, as opposed to waiting to grade the homework to see where they might be at."

—CINDY SCHEUER, TEACHER

One of the most important things we can do with students is to sit down next to them. Doing so strengthens our relationships with students and provides the personalized instruction and feedback that helps them thrive.

NURTURE CREATORS, NOT CONSUMERS

The Internet offers a treasure trove of ideas, resources, opinions, and how-tos (as well as cat memes, ridiculous YouTube videos, and other things that make us smile). The Internet is what it is because people *created*, not because they consumed. If people weren't willing to put themselves and their ideas out for public consumption, this vast resource that we all rely upon so heavily never would have taken off.

Many employers will be looking for creators, for people who are willing to make something that helps others. We can help prepare students to be successful in the marketplace by letting them create in the classroom. Aside from the value they get out of practicing the skill of creating and sharing their creations, students are more engaged in learning when they are creating. This kind of learning feels personal to them. The class becomes more student-centered, which frees the teacher to support and encourage students. Plus, the students will have something to show for their hard work that's more important to them than a worksheet or a sloppily written essay.

STUDENT EXAMPLE

Ella D., Ella H., and Yulia, students in California, created "multiple music" to show how multiples work and to contrast them with a greatest common factor. They created an audio track that played different sounds every two, three, four, five, six and seven seconds to illustrate multiples.

See Ella's blog post and hear their work:
DitchThatHomework.com/multiplemusic

Looking for some ideas on what students can create? Start by heading back to Chapter 2 with ideas for ditching worksheets and research papers. Also, Alice wrote a blog post gathering educators' ideas for upgrading the traditional brochure project. See the crowd-sourced list of ideas and add your own at DitchThatHomework.com/alternatives.

WHAT CAN STUDENTS CREATE?

Website

Podcast

Comic strip

Advertisement

Emoji poetry

Ebook

Magazine cover

Stop-motion animation

Infographic

Icons by Ruslan Dezign, Alfa Design, Jamison Wieser, b farias, Elisabeth Hass, Weltenraser, Andrey Vasiliev, Ilsur Aptukov, Oliviu Stoian via TheNounProject.com

DITCH THAT HOMEWORK

MAKE THE IN-CLASS FLIP

There's been a lot of talk about the concept of flipped classrooms lately. If you aren't familiar with the idea, flipping a classroom is often done when students gather information outside of class and do their work in class. The promise of a flipped classroom is opportunity for the teacher to spend more time on high order skills and activities during class time rather than dispensing information that can be recorded in a video.

But what happens when students don't take the time to prepare for class with the work at home?

Rather than sending students home to learn, we encourage you to consider the *in-class flip* (also called blended learning). In this model, students don't learn outside of class and practice in it. Rather, they learn through bite-sized, on-demand videos, text, graphics, or other mediums besides directly from the teacher. Students engage in collaborative tasks where they start doing something with the information immediately while the teacher engages with students individually as needed. This independent, student-centered learning allows students to work at their own pace and still have access to their teachers. The in-class flip is less focused on location and more focused on activities and access to information. Jason Appel, a math teacher in Rhode Island, explains how this works in his class:

> *I stopped assigning homework last year. We are 1:1 with Chromebooks. I create playlists for every high school geometry lesson. They include videos, Khan Academy practice (DOK 1 and 2), and problem-solving applications (DOK 2 and 3). The tool I use, Formative (goformative.com), provides instant feedback to students on nearly everything they do.*

THE IN-CLASS FLIP

Student learns with bite-sized video

Elements of the in-class flip can be used in any order and in any amount. It empowers students and frees up the teacher to interact one-on-one with students.

Student checks in with teacher for one-on-one coaching

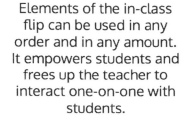

Students start using new info immediately by collaborating

Struggling students get support through targeted videos

Students give and receive feedback

Students create using new info

Thriving students level their work up

Student gets new information through text and graphics

Icons: Jesus Jezzini De Anda, Gerald Wildmoser, Delwar Hossain, Llisole, Arafat Uddin, Amy Morgan, Anbileru Adaleru, Rihards Gromuls via TheNounProject.com

DITCH THAT HOMEWORK

> *Students work through each unit at their own pace.
> They typically work bell to bell just about every day.
> Most students need to do very little work outside of the
> classroom because they make such good use of their time
> in class. If they need extra practice or more time to prog-
> ress through the playlists, they may decide to work on
> them at home.*

Jason's model is packed with great practices: student-centric learning, instant feedback, and access to information at the point of need. He even taps into the students' vocabulary and concepts they're familiar with by creating "playlists" instead of activity lists. You can learn more about Jason's classroom at jasonkappel.com/blog.

Give Choices

Students have a variety of interests, and there's huge power in bringing those interests into the classroom. Incorporating student interests into assignments and classroom activities is a good first step; however, if we gear an individual lecture or homework assignment toward a single student's interest, we assume that every student is alike.

> IF WE GEAR AN INDIVIDUAL LECTURE OR HOMEWORK ASSIGNMENT TOWARD A SINGLE STUDENT'S INTEREST, WE ASSUME THAT EVERY STUDENT IS ALIKE.

Giving students the ability to choose how they demonstrate their learning gives students a locus of control. Having the freedom to make even simple choices, like where to find information and whether to discuss in groups of two or three, gives them a sense of ownership in their learning. With their teacher's guidance, students can learn to make better choices or refine the choices they've already made.

> "Funny thing is, since I have given students choice in what they read and write, students often give themselves homework because they are engaged in their learning."
>
> —PAM GOWER, TEACHER

That ownership of learning prepares them for life beyond the classroom. If they're used to identifying and making their own decisions in school, they'll be more prepared to do that kind of problem-solving outside of school—before *and* after graduation. Choosing how to demonstrate learning, in a small way, helps prepare them to choose a house to buy, formulate a plan of attack for a project at work, and discover how to mend a struggling relationship. When students are accustomed to taking ownership over their own lives in small ways now, it will feel more natural when the big decisions come along.

When students have a say in what they're doing, they get passionate about their work. They are more likely to create something that they'll want to share with others, and they're likely to want to work on it outside of school. Homework they assign to themselves because they love it? That's the best kind of homework. Don't we, as adults, assign ourselves "homework" all the time in our hobbies and

PROVIDE CHOICE

(1) USE THEIR OWN PHOTO

Instead of teacher chosen clip-art, student can customize their assignment with their own picture of image choice.

(2) #1-10 OR #11-20

Giving students choice doesn't have to be complicated. Even simple choices give students a sense of autonomy.

(3) TOOL CHOICE

Allow students to pick which medium they will use to demonstrate the learning objective.

(4) USE CHOICE CENTERS

Choice centers allow students to get up and move and try different activities. Require 3 of the 4 for example.

(5) PICK YOUR POISON

Many students will embrace a tough challenge if they can do it instead of the regular assignment.

(6) SUCCESS BUILDS SUCCESS

Think of your lowest and highest students in the room. Can they be successful and challenged with this assignment?

Icons: Gregor Cresnar, Kirby Wu, Hopkins, ImageCatalog, Arthur Shlain, Peter K. via TheNounProject.com

DITCH THAT HOMEWORK

free-time activities? "Informal learning is a significant aspect of our learning experience," writes George Siemens. "Formal education no longer comprises the majority of our learning. Learning now occurs in a variety of ways—through communities of practice, personal networks, and through completion of work-related tasks" (Siemens 2014).

Why not give your students the same opportunity to pursue their interests? The activities they work on in your classroom may well spark a passion that flourishes into a career or life mission.

DITCH THAT HOMEWORK RESOURCES

As a math teacher, I (Alice) might assign a set of problems from a textbook. An easy way to start offering students choices is to allow the students to choose which problems they want to do.

Or take choice a step further by creating a gamified spreadsheet with a list of choices. In the spreadsheet template, create a list of challenges or options for students. Add a fun title and assign experience points (XP) to each challenge to allow the student to "level up" in the challenge. Set up the spreadsheet so that badges appear when students mark off the choices they've accomplished.

Gamified Student Choice Spreadsheet Template with Badges: DitchThatHomework.com/gamepd

DITCH THAT HOMEWORK RESOURCES

Teacher Jim Bentley says, "In math, I've sometimes asked students to identify four problems that look easy to do, three that look moderately challenging, and two they're unsure about but are willing to try. I'll spend a few minutes with them on the two they were unsure about and then ask them to work on the others individually. When they finish, they check work using an answer key to get quick feedback and meet with me if they need further coaching."

Jim Bentley Select and Choose Template:
DitchThatHomework.com/selectchoose

No one wants to play a video game that is too hard or too easy. When we offer a single option for demonstrating learning, it may be too hard for some or too easy for others. Consider each student in the class. I (Alice) recommend having a spreadsheet with a roster of your students and considering each student and asking, *"How well does my assignment fit this student?"*

The power of technology is one option to make offering choices more feasible. Tech allows us to differentiate assignments and how we expose students to content. Choice could mean many different things:

- Students can choose how they demonstrate their understanding (writing, video, audio, design, etc.).

- Students can choose where they go to gather information (news articles, YouTube, resources in the classroom, etc.).

- Students can choose how they interact with experts and other learners (face-to-face, in comments, through creation, etc.).

We've known for years that students learn differently. Today, we are more empowered than ever to empower students to learn in ways that best suit them.

> **TIP:** Rather than focusing on what assignments you want students to do, consider providing students the learning objective. There are many ways to demonstrate understanding of a learning objective. When students know what they are trying to show, it opens up the possibility for different choices in how they demonstrate their learning.

ENGAGE STUDENTS TO REDUCE HOMEWORK

Picture it: Students are excited about getting started on work in class. They feel like their work is tied to things they're passionate about. They get to choose the kind of work that shows their learning. They're making something instead of just hearing about what they're learning. They're empowered, and they're getting the practice that they need.

Does that sound like the kind of class in which you'd like to learn?

When you mix these ingredients together to create solid learning, it won't be necessary to send home repetitive, shallow worksheets to drive home lessons. Choice, creativity, and personal interest help ensure engagement. And engagement locks in learning. When that happens, you can stop relying on homework. In fact, you may discover you can ditch it all together.

CHAPTER 3
Ditch That Referral

> BUILDING RELATIONSHIPS
> WITH STUDENTS THAT PAY
> DIVIDENDS FOR EVERYONE

DO YOU REMEMBER WHAT LIFE WAS LIKE FOR YOU IN MIDDLE SCHOOL AND HIGH SCHOOL? It's during these turbulent years that, as humans, we try to form our own identities. Maybe you remember how unsure you felt of yourself and your decisions during this time when *everything* was changing, from your growing body to your growing cognitive capacity to your wildly fluctuating hormones. Then, there's the challenge of maintaining delicate relationships with friends, family, and teachers. *Whew!*

Life is just as complicated for students today. It's even more challenging for those whose home lives are affected by bad decisions of the adults in their lives.

For a student, a solid relationship with a trustworthy adult is a lighthouse in a tumultuous sea of uncertainty, which means that one of the most important things we can do, as educators, is build positive relationships with students—the kind of relationships that make kids *want* to come to class.

Believe it or not, homework can be a barrier to those crucial teacher-student relationships. When students don't complete their work or are confused about the work, often the last thing they want to do is come to class. They may even fake being sick or simply skip school because they don't have their homework done. Think about the impact of those missed days! As educators, we know that one of the most important factors to student improvement and learning is attendance.

Sometimes, students don't complete their homework because they didn't understand how to do the task. Sometimes, poorly worded directions leave students at a loss. Other times, kids forget about the assignment or simply opt not to do it because they didn't have enough time or just didn't want to do it.

Regardless of the reason for not doing the homework, when it is an essential part of the lesson and students don't do it, there's going to be a gap in what they know and what they should know. The best way to close that gap is for them to be in class. So if we know that not doing their homework keeps some kids from coming to class but we assign it anyway, we are, in a sense, setting them up for failure.

We (Alice and Matt) want our students to be in class—every day. We bet you feel the same way. As educators, we all want to create the conditions for success by making sure students understand the material and by helping them develop a growth mindset and a love for learning. But we can only do that if they're *in class*. So, instead of writing a disciplinary referral, try ditching it with some of these ideas.

Increase Buy-in with Parents!

"Hi, this is your child's math teacher…" The first time I (Alice) make a call like this, I can hear the wind being sucked out of the person on the other end of the phone.

Many times, when a teacher calls a parent, it's to tattle on the student for misbehavior or incomplete homework. No wonder calls home can create hostility between parents and their children—and between the teacher and the parents and students. I now know that the time I spent calling parents about homework could have been better spent calling them to report positive things about the students or to strategize individualized solutions for struggling students.

What we really want is for students to *understand* the concepts we're teaching. We want them to know how our lessons apply to life (not just the classroom). The end goal isn't simply for kids to collect points; it's to develop skills that will serve them in the future.

> "The first week of school, I email every single parent a positive email about their child. Even with the most challenging child, there is always SOMETHING positive to say! We shouldn't only be sending home negative notes or making negative calls. Parents love to hear great things about their kids, and it helps foster a strong parent/teacher relationship when the teacher isn't ONLY reporting the negatives."
>
> —Karen Mensing, first and second grade teacher

DITCH THAT HOMEWORK RESOURCES

Want to keep better track of the positive conversations you have with parents? We've created this parent/guardian contact log to make your life easier. It will even email parents a copy of what was discussed in the call!

1. Create a copy of the template.

2. Use the Add-on menu to choose "Guardian log" to start the log.

3. Authorize the Add-on script.

4. Add student names and guardian contact information to the tab labeled "Contact Sheet."

5. On the "Contact" tab, enter in the SID or unique student identifier to bring up contact information and fill out the contact form.

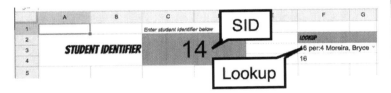

Note: Option to look up the student from a drop down list. Click "Lookup" in the sidebar.

6. In the sidebar, choose "Log Contact" to record notes to the "Contact Log."

Log Contact

It is **important** to log the feedback by clicking the button below.

Log Contact   Log & Calendar

7. Send a contact receipt to either the parent or admin by using the sidebar to choose "Send Parent Contact Receipt" or "Email Admin Contact Receipt."

Email Parent

Email parent a copy of the entry.

Send Parent Contact Receipt

Email admin a copy of the entry.

Email Admin Contact Receipt

When contacting parents, focus on strategies for helping the student progress. Make notes on the first tab of the spreadsheet. The log will show you a list of past parental contacts. If you need to follow up after you contact the parent, use the log to set up a connection to your Google Calendar. Automatically post a follow-up reminder to Google Calendar when logging a contact.

Parent/Guardian Log:
DitchThatHomework.com/parentlog

If we want students to learn and parents to support that learning, they need to buy into the importance of the learning (not one-size-fits-all homework). One of the best ways to get students and parents to buy in is to improve our relationships with them.

(Now, before you think we've gone too touchy-feely, hear us out!)

Put yourself in the shoes of your students' parents. (If you're already a parent, this should be easy. You probably have some experiences with this!) Imagine that your son or daughter has a teacher who has what you believe are unreasonable demands on your child—the activities in class are extremely hard, the comments to your child seem too harsh, the homework load is too heavy, etc.

Can you encourage your child, with conviction, to stay dedicated to this class because it will benefit him/her in the long run? If you have no real relationship with the teacher, your answer would probably be "no." You'd be inclined to believe that the teacher is just exerting his or her power and demanding more than is reasonable just to maintain that sense of power.

Now, imagine that your son or daughter has a teacher with a vision. That teacher has shared the vision with you. You understand that all of the class activities and all of the teacher's feedback are crafted toward helping your child achieve goals you believe in.

What does your support for your child look like with this teacher?

The big difference between these two teachers is the parent/teacher relationship. When the parents are on board at home, it's pretty evident in the results at school. Developing and nurturing positive parent/teacher relationships isn't just "touchy-feely." It's a way to help ensure student success.

Improve Relationship with Students

Just as teachers need to build relationships with parents to get buy-in, we also must develop meaningful connections with our students. The late Rita Pierson, a forty-year classroom veteran, gave one of the best TED Talks we have seen for educators, titled "Every Kid Needs a Champion." In it she shares why positive relationships between teachers and students are so important. (See it at DitchThatHomework.com/champion)

> *James Comer says that no significant learning can occur without a significant relationship. George Washington Carver says all learning is understanding relationships.*

Everyone in this room has been affected by a teacher or an adult. For years, I have watched people teach. I have looked at the best, and I've looked at some of the worst.

A colleague said to me one time, "They don't pay me to like the kids. They pay me to teach a lesson. The kids should learn it. I should teach it; they should learn it. Case closed."

Well, I said to her, "You know, kids don't learn from people they don't like."

She said, "That's just a bunch of hooey."

And I said to her, "Well, your year is going to be long and arduous, dear."

That statement from Rita has stuck with me (Matt) for years.

KIDS DON'T LEARN FROM PEOPLE THEY DON'T LIKE.

Disagree? I did, too, early in my teaching career. At that point, I knew what kids needed and I had plans to give it to them. If they didn't like it, they were going to have to deal with it.

My attitude provoked lots of arguments. In essence, I chose to stand toe-to-toe with teenagers, daring them to back down. (Sometimes, I did this in the middle of class, which led to the whole class standing up to me for their friend … not the best atmosphere for learning!) They couldn't do what I asked? I viewed those students' circumstances as a poor excuse. If they didn't understand my lesson, it was probably because they weren't trying hard enough.

Relationships are enormously important to students, and I learned this in a way I didn't expect. From time to time, I (Matt) had students do blatantly disrespectful and disruptive things in class. They would say inappropriate words, mutter snide comments about their classmates, and make all of the loud body noises they could. I couldn't fathom why they would do that when they *knew* it would lead to discipline. Then, immediately after, I would see them sneak a glance at someone out of the corner of their eye. *Ah*, I would think, *there it is.* The discipline was the last thing on their mind. Misguided or not, they thought doing that stuff would make them look cool and, in turn, improve their relationships with their friends.

Relationships are a huge part of their lives—maybe *the* most important part. They would put themselves in harm's way—or risk disciplinary action—to improve their standing in the eyes of their friends. And I was totally ignoring the relationship aspect of teaching.

I wasn't seeing my students as people, as unique human beings. I was seeing them as soldiers that needed to fall in line.

When my approach changed, my relationships with my students changed. And I noticed a change in their learning. When they saw that they mattered in my eyes, that I cared about who they were as people, suddenly, it wasn't me versus them. They started to come over to my side, and they were more likely to give me the benefit of the doubt because I wasn't their adversary; I was their advocate. And over time, the improved relationships with my students led to improved learning.

So how can you build better relationships with your students and their parents? We have some ideas.

CHANGE CONVERSATIONS

When I (Alice) stopped assigning homework, my conversations with students changed. The discussions about why their homework wasn't done stopped—because there was no homework to do. By eliminating homework, I eliminated a major source of hostility in my classroom.

I've mentioned that a typical lesson for me during my early years of teaching was to start class by going over the homework. "Going over the homework" meant that I was talking while the students looked over their homework, if they did it. I had students who neglected to do the assignment, lined up at the phone calling their parents to tattle on themselves while I collected and recorded work. After my homework "talk," I talked some more, this time about a math problem that students would copy down, along with the steps to solving it. After a little guided practice (more talking on my part), students had a few minutes to work on their homework at the end of class.

How many minutes did *I* spend talking? A lot.

How many minutes did *each student* get to talk? Very few.

How many minutes was I able to sit next to a student and give feedback? Only a few minutes at the end.

In this model, when students needed help while they were doing the work, I wasn't there—because almost all the work was done (or not done) at home. During the time we spent together in class, I talked *at* the students, not *with* them.

When I stopped assigning homework, the conversations became more meaningful because they were about *learning*. We talked about why a new concept didn't make sense. I helped them figure out the answers for themselves. And I encouraged them when they made a breakthrough.

How do we improve relationships with students? For one, start class by having positive conversations with students. Instead of asking kids why they didn't do their homework, ask about what students are into. Ask what they're excited about right now and what they're going to do tonight after school or this weekend.

Is all that talk a waste of time? Nope. It's an investment in effective instruction. Knowing what makes your students tick can be invaluable to connect learning to their interests. If we really want to make that investment work for us, we must use what we learn—in our interactions with students and in our instruction.

CHANGE THE WAY STUDENTS ASK QUESTIONS

While we're changing conversations, let's change how students ask for help. Many students are more likely to ask a question or indicate they are struggling if they can ask digitally. In general, students feel more confident asking a question through an email or an instant message to the teacher or posting a question on a discussion board than they do raising a hand to ask a question. To some students, the attention that comes from asking a question is mortifying enough to keep them from doing it. Asking questions digitally lets the student get the answer without risking embarrassment.

ASK FOR FEEDBACK

When is the last time you filled out a customer service survey? Many companies, such as banks and restaurants, ask for feedback after every single visit. They use that data to make changes and improvements for their customers. Maybe that's not a bad idea.

Think of teaching as a customer service job. What if you considered that your students are your customers and periodically asked what they thought of their learning experience? What kind of feedback do you think you'd get? It may sound a little scary, but having used this approach ourselves, we can tell you that the information you'll get when you ask students for input can be invaluable.

Your "survey" doesn't have to be complex. Try using a digital tool to ask for student feedback on each lesson. (Simple slips of paper work just as effectively.) Then, take what you learn and use it to start meaningful conversations. Those conversations can help you build relationships which will help you identify and assist struggling students.

DITCH THAT HOMEWORK RESOURCES

Teachers have lots of options for digital platforms to survey students on how they feel about their learning. Among them are private comments in Google Classroom, Google Forms, your school or district's learning-management system, setting up a Padlet board (padlet.com), and any quiz tool. (Check the link below for a few sample questions you can ask your students.) Use the student feedback to help improve your lesson planning. We always get better with feedback.

Sample Exit Ticket Question:
DitchThatHomework.com/exitticket

  Krista Weller
2:20 PM

#058 Exit Ticket - Customer Satisfaction Survey

Click on Open
In the private comments please indicate
"What questions do you have?"
"What did you feel most successful at today?"
"What do you need further practice with?"
"What would you like to communicate to the teacher?"

Exit Ticket

Stop ... Collaborate and Listen

As digital communication improves, the world continues to feel smaller and more connected. Social media and smartphones allow us to send instant messages to practically anyone at any time. We can see and hear friends, family members, and colleagues all over the world with Skype or FaceTime calls.

As the capabilities of our communication tools expand, so will the need for teamwork and collaboration skills. The National Association of Colleges and Employers (NACE) publishes its annual Job Outlook, which includes a list of sought-after skills for job candidates. Included in that list for 2013, in order of importance, are the following skills (*DitchThatHomework.com/2013skills*):

- Ability to work in a team (No. 1)
- Ability to make decisions and solve problems (No. 2)
- Ability to communicate verbally with people inside and outside an organization (No. 4)
- Ability to sell and influence others (No. 10)

In 2016, NACE updated its list. Working in a team dropped to No. 2. Decision-making and problem-solving dropped to No. 4. Communicating verbally dropped to No. 5. So these communication skills are losing their value? Not exactly. New to the top five were leadership (No. 1) and written communication skills (No. 3) (*DitchThatHomework.com/2016skills*).

Communication and collaboration are key in today's workforce—and tomorrow's.

Innovative companies from every industry are trying to create the best products for their users. Technology companies, like Google and Apple, are known for their commitment to seeking out the best ideas

THE VALUE OF
COMMUNICATION
AND
COLLABORATION

" Which skills are most important in job candidates? "

2013		2016
10	Leadership / influence others	1
2	Ability to work in a team	2
--	Communication skills (written)	3
3	Problem-solving skills	4
1	Communication skills (verbal)	5
4	Ability to plan, organize and prioritize work	--
5	Ability to obtain and process information	--

Icon by Rick Pollock via TheNounProject.com Source: NACE Job Outlook 2013 and 2016 (naceweb.org)

51

through collaboration. Do you think leaders at Google worry about who came up with a great idea? Do they ask their employees, "Did you do this by yourself, without looking at your colleagues' screens?"

No way! Google's leaders know that the company thrives, and its customers are better served when its employees work together. It's like the saying that's circulating widely in education circles: "The smartest person in the room is the room." When we communicate and collaborate effectively and often, it shows and we produce our best work. This must show up in the classroom.

Maintaining positive student relationships doesn't stop with the student/teacher connection. When we help students improve relationships with one another, they get valuable practice for life in the real world. Plus, when students are able to resolve conflicts on their own, many of the distractions that prevent learning are eliminated.

Strengthening student-to-student relationships is such foundational work in Paul Solarz's classroom that it starts on the first day of school. In his student-led fifth-grade class, students can stop everything and call everyone's attention if they need to. They make suggestions on lessons. They help one another solve problems and stay on task.

"I plan out the lessons and the curriculum because that's my expertise," said Solarz. "But I have the kids doing things like getting the computer cart out, taking care of the classroom, managing materials, and collaborating with each other when they're confused."

His student-led class loses focus, momentum, and learning time if the students don't respect one another. "I need to build relationships with students, but they need to build relationships with each other, too," he said. "I need every kid to work with every kid to build those relationships, especially if they've had a bad relationship in the past."

What's the effect of those improved student-to-student relationships? Personality conflicts don't derail a class. Students know that they're appreciated in a time of life that causes so much uncertainty. And they are better prepared for their future, where building and maintaining relationships will be a huge asset in their personal and professional lives.

All in all, time spent on improving relationships—with parents, with students and student-to-student—improves learning in the long run. Those solid relationships build the foundation that your educational house rests on—and wards off the cracks that cause things to crumble.

CHAPTER 4
Ditch That Resistance

THROUGH THE YEARS, WE'VE HEARD A FEW PARENTS TRY TO EXPLAIN WHY THEY THINK HOMEWORK IS CRUCIAL. There's always the "it helped us to be successful" rationalization and the "it teaches responsibility" reason. But one particular argument frustrates us more than all the others: "*Homework helps us know what's going on in our kid's classroom.*"

When we hear parents say this, it evokes a few emotions: frustration, sadness, and disappointment.

Here's why: Many times, parents aren't really saying they want their kids to do more school work at home. They're just crying out to be involved in their child's education.

DITCH THAT HOMEWORK RESOURCES

Learning together can be the catalyst to quality family time. Encourage parents to ask questions, use an image to spark a conversation, or pull out a puzzle to get the whole family working and learning together.

In addition to tried-and-true activities such as counting circles, number talks, and noticings and wonderings, a wealth of resources are available to parents who want to challenge their children's thinking. For example, check out tabletalkmath.com/resources, where parents (and educators) can explore a variety of prompts and ideas. You can also sign up for a free newsletter with quick ways to engage in math conversations around the dinner table or in the car on the way to school (available in English and Spanish).

Most parents understand the importance of education. They know that education is critical to their children's future success, and they want to do their best to help their children succeed. When they see their children studying at home, they feel better about what's going on in school. For some parents, homework is one of the few ways they learn about and get to participate in what's being taught in the classroom.

Frankly, we think assigning homework is a rotten way to communicate with parents.

> FRANKLY, WE THINK ASSIGNING HOMEWORK IS A ROTTEN WAY TO COMMUNICATE WITH PARENTS.

WORKING HAND IN HAND WITH PARENTS

Any academic work students do should benefit *them*. It isn't for the parents. It's to help students to grow, develop, learn, and improve their skills.

That said, we can't leave parents on the sidelines. At least, we shouldn't. Parents can be the greatest advocates for our students' success—at home *and* at school. Rather than relegating their involvement to going over worksheets or working on projects that they don't value, parents should be part of a child's learning support system—every day. And that requires good teacher/parent/student communication.

Good communication doesn't happen in just one parent-teacher meeting per year. Sending a link to your website or class newsletter is a decent start, but it's a drop in a bucket that should be filled with meaningful, personal communication. Instead of putting more time into assigning and collecting homework, a better investment in student success is spending time communicating with parents.

LET PARENTS INSIDE THE CLASSROOM VIRTUALLY

With all of the communication tools available today, it's fairly simple to find a method that will work for you and your students' parents. Take a look at these examples:

- **Create a class social media account**. Post big, important messages *and* little, day-to-day happenings on it. Post pictures of what's going on in class. Share videos of students working on projects or doing presentations. Post students quotes—the funny, witty, interesting, quotable things students say. (Be sure to get their permission first.) Post regularly, and let students post, too! If you're unsure about which social media to choose, ask parents which one they use the most. (Hint: As of the publication of this book, Facebook is popular with many parents. Instagram is gaining ground, and Snapchat is becoming more widely used.) Want an example to follow? Check out Kayla Delzer's class accounts where her third graders post regularly. They're on Twitter (*twitter.com/TopDogKids*), Instagram (*instagram.com/topdogkids*) and Snapchat (*@topdogkids*).

- **Use parent communication tools**. Various apps and websites help keep parents and teachers in touch, giving families a window into the classroom. Remind (remind.com) lets teachers broadcast text messages to parents, students, and others. Teachers can use it to send assignment and test reminders, and they can use the service to text every parent at once with little peeks into what students are doing in the classroom. Remind also offers two-way Facebook Messenger-style communication between parents and teachers. Bloomz (bloomz.net) lets teachers share class updates by text, photo or video with parents. It also helps coordinate reminders, parent-teacher conferences and volunteer sign-ups. It may seem obvious that parents of elementary school students would want regular updates, but parents of older students also want to be kept in the loop. (What parent doesn't need a good topic of conversation with their kids?!)

- **Send personalized email newsletters**. Email newsletters are good, but their reach can be limited. Busy parents tend to not read them if there's nothing personal or specific to their children. Now, with tools such as Autocrat or the Teacher Newsletter add-on, it's easy to create custom email newsletters for parents. Curious about how it works? Watch a tutorial video on creating a custom email newsletter with Autocrat at *DitchThatHomework.com/autocratnewsletter*, and visit *DitchThatHomework.com/teachernewsletter* to see how to use the Teacher Newsletter add-on.

- **Distribute a parent survey**. Surveys make it easy for parents to submit feedback and share their ideas. Use short surveys to ask parents anything you'd like to know—from struggles their kids are having with classwork, to how their child feels about school, to issues at home you should know about, etc. Create a simple survey in Google Forms and email it to parents. If you send out surveys regularly, parents will expect them and get in the habit of responding. Once you get feedback from parents, do something with it. Otherwise, parents may feel as if completing the survey is an exercise in futility. Also, consider identifying people who contribute ideas that lead to change. A simple "Thanks to Sydney's parents' ideas, we're starting this" can go a long way.

Once you've shown parents what's going on in the classroom, empower them to help their students succeed. When parents know what students are working on—and how it ties into their everyday lives at home—they can reinforce the concepts being covered in class. Use those channels of communication (social media, blogs, newsletters, etc.) to show parents how to incorporate lesson material into conversations at dinner, while watching TV, in the car, or while having fun with their kids.

"I still have parents who want to work with their kids on academics. I am not assigning paper worksheets, but I do give parents access to games they can play with their kids if they want to practice skills with them (e.g., multiplication games they can play to practice facts if desired.). My parents were concerned about no homework. I came to Meet the Teacher Night prepared with studies and articles about the impact of homework at the elementary school level."

—LESA HANEY, TEACHER

HELP PARENTS GET ON BOARD

When communicating with parents about your decision to ditch (or reduce) homework, be sure to share your vision. Reassure parents by explaining how you plan to help students succeed without them having to take home much work. Whether you're making the shift mid-year or are beginning a new school year with a homework-free syllabus, good communication (again) is the best tool you have to gaining parental support.

Perhaps you've seen a few of the letters from teachers to parents about eliminating homework circulating on social media. In these letters, the teachers typically write about what changes are taking place, explain why they're happening, and dispel any disagreements or doubts.

Those letters are well-intentioned, and they're much better than instituting a policy without any notice. We want to encourage you to take your communication a step further, though: Try to talk to every child's parents.

Yes, it takes a lot of extra effort. Some parents will seem impossible to reach. But connecting with parents individually is worth the effort. We're not telling you that you *must* talk to parents of each and every child before you stop assigning homework. But if you want each student to have his or her best chance at success, the more supporters you have the better. Any bit of dissent in one household can trickle and spread to other families through social media, text messages, or conversations at extra-curricular activities.

Your best chance at helping doubtful or unsure parents is through eye-to-eye, voice-to-voice, heart-to-heart conversations. Phone calls are the next best option. Emails and paper fliers are efficient but lack the personal touch of a voice. When you're speaking to your students' parents, consider using the following ideas to help them get on board:

- **Help them see your vision**. Ask them, "What would life be like if your child had less homework? What would you be able to do with the extra time?" Or, if you don't want to ask, describe the vision in your own words. "Imagine life with less homework. You're able to ___. You finally have time to ___." (Persuasion experts suggest that you not ask a question you don't know the answer to, so if you're unsure how a parent will react, try describing the benefits instead of asking.)

- **Share your heart**. Let them know why you're passionate or excited about this change. Show them that you're convinced and confident. When you share your positive, authentic emotions, you will connect with the parents' hearts.

- **Cite research that supports your decision**. Even though many homework studies have their flaws (as we discussed in the introduction), research can go a long way to convince parents. Don't get overly technical, and don't inundate them with too much. Pick one or two studies that support your point of view. (We shared several points in this book's introduction.)

- **Point to your own experiences**. Personal stories can be powerful. If you've seen the inadequacies or inefficiencies of homework as a teacher, parent, or student, share them. Sharing your experiences often helps parents understand how much you have in common with one another.

- **Give them plenty of opportunity to talk**. They may have questions. Answer them as honestly as possible. If you don't know the answer, promise to find the answer and reconnect with them at a later time. (And then do it!) They may just want to talk—to describe their concerns, their fears, and their own stories. Sometimes, a listening ear does more to convince someone than 100 valid reasons ever could. When parents raise an objection with a teacher, what they are really saying is, "This isn't working for my kid." Are you willing to come up with a plan and make adjustments or do you just want parents to know how their child can be compliant?

- **Don't overdo it**. Be concise. State your case plainly, then see what they have to say. We have all had someone make a lengthy, long-winded case to us when we had our minds made up in the first thirty seconds. Try to make the conversation a dialogue rather than a monologue.

Are you concerned about finding time to make all of those personal contacts? Consider a week of assignments in class where the work isn't collected and graded by you. That should free you up enough to make some calls or see parents face-to-face. This is also a great strategy to use for freeing up time to make positive calls and emails to parents as well. Back-to-school night or parent-teacher conferences, of course, are also excellent opportunities to talk to parents face-to-face.

DITCH THAT HOMEWORK RESOURCES

We conducted a survey of parents on their attitudes and beliefs about homework. It was not designed to be scientific—just a Google Forms survey distributed through our email lists and social media. We received almost 800 responses, and many of the stories and comments shared in the survey are included throughout this book. Here are some of the findings: ⟶

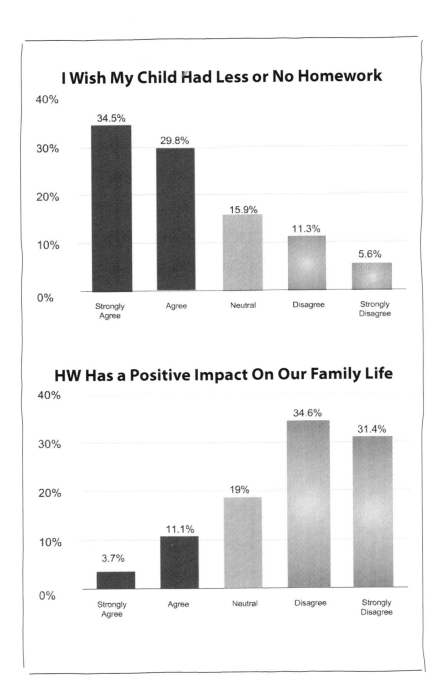

I Wish My Child Had Less or No Homework

HW Has a Positive Impact On Our Family Life

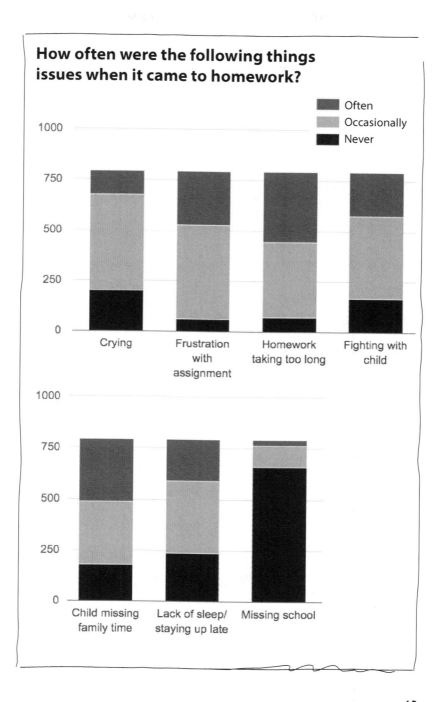

How often were the following things issues when it came to homework?

Keep It in Perspective

As educators, our decisions regarding homework affect not just our students but all the families they represent. And those families comprise different dynamics, different socioeconomic and education levels, different personalities, and different values. So if not everyone jumps on board with your vision right away, don't take it personally. As you interact with parents, it always helps to keep a clear perspective.

If you get some resistance, don't let it shake your resolve. Remember that the squeaky wheel gets the grease. Are you hearing one wheel squeak or all of them? Take a look at Facebook. If your feed is like ours, you'll see more parents stressing over their child's workload than parents bemoaning the lack of rigorous homework being sent home. Do you hear a fellow teacher or an administrator say, "Parents are demanding regular homework!" Ask, "How many?" You might also ask, "How many parents are begging for less homework?" Squeaky wheels can make a lot of noise; don't assume one voice is more important than the others just because it's loud.

Parents have great insight that we don't have as teachers. My wife and I (Matt) have taken our children to quite a few pediatricians and doctors. In several instances, those doctors have used our observations about our children to determine a diagnosis. They're the ones with the degree in medicine and years of experience. Why would they consider our opinion on our children's care?

One doctor explained it this way. He said, "You're with your children all the time—a lot more than me. You know what normal looks like. You know when something isn't right. Why wouldn't I use that?"

If doctors do that with medical diagnoses, why wouldn't we do that with class assignments?

> IF DOCTORS DO THAT WITH MEDICAL DIAGNOSES, WHY WOULDN'T WE DO THAT WITH CLASS ASSIGNMENTS?

In the same way with homework, honor parents who say, "This wasn't appropriate for my child." If you don't differentiate, consider letting the parent help. Remember: Parents want to be involved. They have their children's best interests at heart. We're all on the same team, and we all want to see children succeed. If we can partner with parents to find the best method for student learning, we may discover a method together that we couldn't individually.

At some point, though, a line has to be drawn between what the parents suggest and what you decide. In the end, you're the highly qualified educator with training in pedagogy, instruction, and curriculum. Use parent input to help the student as long as it's serving the best interest of student learning.

Keep things equitable for all students. It's easy to slip into the mindset that everyone else is like us. As teachers—with college degrees and certificates to practice in our profession—we have a high level of education. (In some areas, teachers are some of the most highly educated people in the community.) As college-educated individuals, we can help our own children with homework if we need to. If we don't remember that particular topic from school, we can find resources to remind us—or to teach us from scratch.

Learning does not come as easily for everyone, and not everyone has the time to spend hours helping their children do their homework every evening. Think of the single parent who works two jobs to keep food on the table. Think of the husband and wife who are barely getting by working alternate shifts. They are lucky if they get a few minutes together a week as a family.

In those households, survival takes precedence over everything, including homework.

Sure, you'll probably have plenty of families who are able to support their children academically. But many families just can't do it for a multitude of reasons (and that doesn't make for bad parents). Children from those families are likely the ones who already have huge obstacles to overcome to succeed. Let's keep everything in perspective and remember that homework can put more obstacles in the way for certain families.

Ditching homework leaves time for extracurricular activities, and that's a good thing. We spend seven hours a day helping students grow and thrive academically. By freeing up time after school for extracurricular activities—sports, band, theater, service projects, etc.—we're helping students become more well-rounded human beings.

The benefits students get from participating in sports, for example, are numerous—and they include academic benefits. In addition to the brain boosting power of physical activity, sports teach kids how to work on a team and how to persist through challenges. As a result, many students demonstrate improvement in academics and an increase in self-confidence and concentration. We've personally seen the difference that involvement in athletics can make in students' well-being, and research supports the benefits of activity and sports. In fact, according to one study, strenuous physical activity improves their academic performance (Sattelmair et al. 2009). Another study, this one by Touch Research Institutes at the University of Miami, states that a high level of exercise has been connected to better parent/child relationships, less depression, and less drug use than those with a less active lifestyle (Field et al. 2001).

Homework causes stress. Physical activity relieves stress. As you're sharing your reasons for ditching homework, remind parents that a well-rounded school experience includes making time for many different kinds of activities. Let's stop giving kids homework so they can choose healthier options.

Parents and teachers have the same goal: helping our children/students succeed. Let's keep in perspective that the demands of our own individual classes aren't the only ones on students and their families. If we take the time to recruit parental support and empower them to help their kids thrive, they can be our biggest allies.

CHAPTER 5
DITCH THOSE HABITS

> ## UNLEASHING POWERFUL, BRAIN-FRIENDLY LEARNING

FOR GENERATIONS, MANY TEACHERS — GOOD, WELL-MEANING TEACHERS — HAVE BEEN GIVING STUDENTS ADVICE ON HOW TO LEARN, STUDY FOR TESTS, AND PREPARE FOR THE FUTURE. Sadly, many of these teachers have been giving bad advice without even realizing it.

Recently, cognitive science has yielded important discoveries from brain scans, studies, and experiments. The findings reveal how the brain works and how it learns best. This research can have a great impact on education. Unfortunately, much of it has yet to be applied in the classroom. That's a shame because making some simple changes in how teachers teach and how students learn could do wonders for efficiency and effectiveness. The good news is that many of these best practices require only small changes to make huge impact on learning and on retention.

And if students learn and retain learning more effectively, dependency on homework will diminish.

RETRIEVAL'S POWERFUL EFFECT ON THE BRAIN

Think for a minute about what your teaching would look like if you didn't have to spend so much time reteaching the same material. Now consider how your students' school experiences (and life experiences!) would be improved if they actually retained information and new ideas long term.

What happens all too often in classrooms around the world is that students are encouraged to reread and memorize material in hope of getting it to solidify in their minds. Students are told to "study"—to read over chapters for a second or third time, to highlight important concepts, to take even more notes.

Surprisingly, research shows that this kind of repetition isn't really effective.

There's a better way to help students remember new material and concepts, and far too few teachers are using it. It's called "retrieval."

Retrieval looks like this: Students study new material (or go back over old material). Every once in a while, they stop studying and retrieve information out of their brains, recalling and restating the new information in their own words. They can ask themselves questions. They can stop and tell someone else. When using retrieval, students stop the active reading or studying of new material. This is more effective than our practice of reading and reading and reading, continually cramming new material into the brain without stopping.

RETRIEVAL: Your brain's strong ally

Learn smarter with less effort the way your brain craves!

Study (new ideas or review)	Stop studying	Retrieve from memory

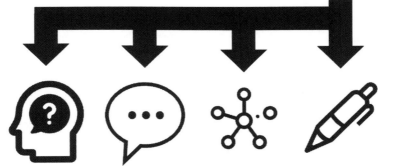

Self-assess with questions	Retell what you remember	Create a mind map	Draw new ideas out

Icons: Dairy Free Design, Chinnaking, Travis Avery, Francesca Arena, Gregor Cresnar, Mert Güler, Vladimir Belochkin, B. Farias via TheNounProject.com.

Resume learning

Teaching students how to retrieve information makes perfect sense. Think about it: When we take tests, this is exactly how we call facts and ideas out of our brains—by retrieving them. Students see a question, and they stop and recall the answer from memory. Retrieval practice in studying is essentially a dress rehearsal for the test. Doesn't it make sense, then, to have students practice that skill?

A study done at Purdue University in West Lafayette, Indiana, shows the benefits of retrieval. In an experiment, two groups of undergraduate students studied a science text in different ways. The first group practiced "elaboration" by reading and creating a concept map to help them remember new ideas. The second group practiced retrieval. Both groups read the material and then stopped to recall as much of what they learned as they could afterward. Study time was exactly the same. The results? Students using retrieval had better scores and a 50 percent improvement in long-term retention (Karpicke et al. 2011).

That's good enough to prove that retrieval works, isn't it? Not so fast. The researchers did a second experiment, putting retrieval at a disadvantage in an attempt to prove its effectiveness. The students prepared for the tests in the same way—one group created concept maps and the other group stopped to recall what they had learned. However, this time, the concept mapping group was given strategies to create better concept maps. Plus, the final test was to create a concept map. This gave the concept mappers a huge advantage over those practicing retrieval—a completely uneven playing field for the retrieval group.

With those advantages given to the concept mapping group, the retrieval group had no chance of winning, right? Think again. Eighty four percent of students (101 out of 120) performed better practicing retrieval instead of elaboration (creating a concept map). It wasn't even close. Retrieval outperformed traditional studying techniques—with one metaphorical hand tied behind its back.

"Retrieval practice produced the best learning, better than elaborative studying with concept mapping, which itself was not significantly better than spending additional time reading," wrote Jeffrey D. Karpicke and Janell R. Blunt of their study.

Retrieval works. So why aren't we using it with students more? Maybe the problem is that not enough teachers know about its effectiveness.

Or maybe the problem is that they don't believe it will work. It's unintuitive. It seems too good to be true—or too easy to be truly effective. The students in the study tended to agree. Before taking the test in the second experiment (the one that gave the elaboration group the advantage of practicing concept maps), the researchers asked students which method would be more effective. Half thought the concept map would better prepare them. Only a quarter expected retrieval to be more effective.

Even if teachers or students have heard of retrieval, they often don't see it as a legit study method. Research tells a different story. Pooja K. Agarwal, a cognitive scientist and former classroom teacher, says there's ample research showing that retrieval can benefit all grade levels, all subject areas, and all students.

What does retrieval look like? It can include closed-ended and multiple choice questions as well as open-ended questions that encourage students to summarize learning. Agarwal offers practical strategies and more information about retrieval at *RetrievalPractice. org*, and here are a few simple ways to incorporate retrieval as a learning strategy in your classroom:

- Encouraging students to stop occasionally while reading or studying to mentally recall what they've learned

- Using quick formative assessment tools, including web tools like Kahoot! or Quizizz

- Creating colored index cards or cards with letters for quick multiple-choice assessment

- Using bell-ringer activities or exit tickets that encourage students to recall what they have learned

THE TRICK TO SPACING AND PACING

I (Matt) remember cramming for way too many tests as a college student. I was a studying procrastinator, and I found that even when I delayed my studying too long, I could usually make up for that procrastination (to some extent, at least) by cramming all night before an exam. I usually did fine on the exam. But if you asked me now about anything I studied in that way, I would have no recollection of it. To be honest, if you asked me two weeks later, I likely wouldn't either.

Here's the problem: I was studying in a way that was convenient for me, but my brain despised it. I commonly used this one-and-done studying that packaged all my learning into one tidy block of time and then moved on.

What the human brain craves *is spaced retrieval*, which occurs when you practice a skill for a time, then set it aside once you get the hang of it, and then pick it back up, retrieving it from your brain again later when the skill starts to feel a little rusty. When you (or your students) use this method over and over and over again, learning *really sticks!*

"Information that is spaced over time is better remembered than the same amount of information massed together," explain researchers at the Rutgers University Department of Psychology and Center for Collaborative Neuroscience (Sisti 2007). Put simply, when we engage in units of study in the classroom for weeks at a time and then move on without looking back, we're putting students at a cognitive disadvantage.

"The principle of mass-practice relies on short-term memory, whereas durable learning requires time for mental rehearsal and the other processes of consolidation to take effect, including forgetting," wrote Jeff Mehring and Regan Thomson in their article "Brain-Friendly Learning Tips for Long-Term Retention and Recall" in *The Language Teacher* (Mehring et al. 2016).

Wait a second. *Forgetting* is an important part of learning? Aren't we supposed to help our students remember and not forget? It turns out that learning *and* forgetting are both important parts of the learning process.

"Conditions that produce forgetting often enable additional learning, and learning or recalling some things can contribute to forgetting other things," wrote Robert A. Bjork in the book *Remembering: Attributions, Processes, and Control in Human Memory* (Bjork 2015).

Here are a few ways to use spaced repetition and forgetting to your students' advantage in the classroom:

- Throw old terms, concepts, and ideas into a review activity.

- Integrate previously covered material with new material in questions and activities.

- Use bell-ringer activities or exit slips to reactivate prior knowledge.

- Play a "What Do You Remember?" review game of previously covered content.

Whatever you do, make sure that end-of-the-year assessments aren't the only time when you go over content that you've covered throughout the year.

SITTING HURTS CHILDREN'S BRAIN FUNCTION

In addition to spaced repetition and retrieval, there's a secret ingredient for boosting students' performance in the classroom. It's available to every teacher and every student. It is free, but many schools are *cutting back on it* instead of adding more.

That ingredient is physical activity.

Kids have lots of energy—much more energy than us adults! They squirm and fidget and talk when they're told to sit down and be quiet.

They all but vibrate with energy, so it isn't surprising to learn that the sedentary nature in many schools is doing considerable harm to children and teens' health. The World Health Organization lists mobility as one of its emerging health issues for children (*DitchThatHomework.com/who*). It cites studies showing a number of concerns:

- Many children consume more calories than they're able to burn in a day.

- Low energy expenditure in children was 200 kilocalories below estimates for their ages. (It would take an eight-year-old boy with average weight of fifty-six pounds an extra hour of basketball, an extra two hours of leisurely cycling, or an extra hour and a half of hopscotch to burn 200 kilocalories.)

Many teachers think they're doing well to encourage students to be quiet, sit still, and work. According to brain research, however, what students really need is *less* time being still and quiet to achieve *more* academically.

For example, researchers Benjamin A. Sibley and Jennifer L. Etnier found that any type of physical activity helps students think more clearly and learn more easily. Their study found that those who benefit the most from physical activity are elementary and middle school students (through eighth grade). However, physical activity helped all levels of students with IQ and academic achievement, according to their research (Sibley and Etnier 2003).

The U.S. National Institutes of Health also support physical activity to promote learning (Kohl and Cook, 2013). Its National Center for Biotechnology Information makes these claims regarding the connection between movement and learning:

- Physical activity/fitness may improve academic performance.

- Daily time dedicated to recess, PE, and physical activity in the classroom may facilitate academic performance.

- Math and reading are topics most influenced by physical activity.

- Given the importance of time on task to learning, students should be provided with frequent physical activity breaks that are developmentally appropriate.

- Although presently understudied, physically active lessons offered in the classroom may increase time on task and attention to task in the classroom setting.

It's odd, then, that some schools ditch physical education and recess in favor of a focus on serious learning. It turns out that sedentary "focus" does more harm than good! Thankfully, teachers have a variety of options when it comes to boosting the physical-activity factor in their classes:

- **Take a walk.** It elevates the heart rate, gets blood pumping, and stimulates brain activity. When I (Matt) struggle with topics for my blog, I'll go for a run. I'll often return to jot new ideas down on a notepad or whiteboard before I forget them all! Similarly, teacher and author Catlin Tucker's students go on an "Instagram sensory walk" (DitchThatHomework.com). They snap pictures along the way and put their senses—especially smells, sounds, and feelings—into words in the photo captions.

"My first year of teaching, I was required to have many observations. After getting dinged for unfocused, chatty kids, I started to take them out for about ten minutes before observations to run. They loved it, and I truly saw classroom focus improve. Kids need to move!"

—KAREN MENSING, FIRST AND SECOND GRADE TEACHER

- **Build some movement into your activities.** Have students get up and move to a different part of the room for each new activity. If they can walk (or hop or do sit-ups or whatever) while they learn, even better! If you've seen *Akeelah and the Bee*, you saw Akeelah doing this while practicing spelling words by tapping letters out on her leg or spelling while jumping rope.

- **Tap into brain break resources like GoNoodle (*gonoodle.com*).** Younger elementary students love GoNoodle videos. Older students can get into them, too, if you model enthusiasm, choose activities carefully, and use GoNoodle items (lanyards, label templates, etc.) creatively.

- **Be willing to trade time.** When I (Matt) had a rambunctious class of freshmen, I found that trading a few minutes of physical activity made them more attentive for the rest of class. I let them run around outside the exterior door right next to my room and, surprisingly, they returned more settled and ready to learn.

Create New, Powerful Habits

We are all creatures of habit, and I (Matt) am one of the worst. I make wrong turns while driving because I go into "autopilot" mode. I'll pull the wrong ingredients out of the refrigerator if I'm not thinking about the recipe I'm working on.

The reason we rely on habitual behaviors, writes Charles Duhigg in his book, *The Power of Habit*, is because it's easier on the brain (Duhigg 2009). The brain wants to take the path of least resistance. Relying on a well-ingrained habit requires far less mental energy than creating a new behavior.

Habits affect everyone in the classroom. Teachers follow instructional patterns in their lessons. They use the same language in prompts and directions, so students process them easier. Habits are also the reason students tend to sit in the same seats, even if they don't have an assigned seating chart.

As teachers, we'd give *a lot* to eliminate bad habits that inhibit learning. For instance, students forget to write down due dates in their planners or to bring important materials to class.

The best way to eliminate a bad habit is to identify it and replace it with a good one, Duhigg explains in *The Power of Habit*. Identifying a bad habit requires understanding the habit loop, a process made up of three steps:

- The Cue (what causes you to act)
- The Routine (what we do when prompted)
- The Reward (the driving force for the action)

If students are failing to write due dates and other important information in their planners, maybe they're missing one of those three important factors:

- The Cue (being prompted by the teacher)
- The Routine (writing it down)
- The Reward (earning better grades)

When you are trying to engineer a positive habit and some parts of the habit loop don't work together, the new habit fails. That's when it's time to start analyzing the parts of the routine. For example, by better understanding the cue, we can figure out what's really triggering the routine. Duhigg identifies five main triggers of habits:

- Location
- Time
- Emotional State
- Other People
- Immediately Preceding Action

As a teacher, you have the opportunity to help students—entire classes of them or individuals—create better habits by making them aware of their behaviors and what drives them. And you may end up creating some positive habits for yourself, as well!

Other Ways to Hack the Brain

"People generally are going about learning in the wrong ways," explains Peter C. Brown and cognitive scientists Henry Roediger and Mark McDaniel in the book, *Make It Stick* (Brown et al. 2014). The most likely reason for this is that scientifically proven methods to achieve better learning and longer retention don't always make sense. They aren't necessarily intuitive, but they work!

Here are some important truths, from *Make it Stick*, that you can use to improve learning in your classroom:

Trying to solve a problem before being taught the solution leads to better learning, even when errors are made in the attempts. The argument against this method sounds something like this: *But what if I let them try it and they mess it up? They'll be creating bad habits*. Brain research proves otherwise. When the brain has to work to figure out a solution, it is better able to remember the problem, the solution, as well as how it was achieved.

If you practice elaboration—giving new material meaning by expressing it in your own words and connecting it with what you already know—there's no known limit to how much you can learn. I think this is why I (Matt) like sketchnoting (aka visual notetaking) so much. I can break down and organize new ideas in a way that makes sense in my brain, and then I have a custom-created visual aid to fall back on.

Learning sinks in when a strong, personal, or concrete connection is made to the material. In the Substitution Augmentation

Modification and Redefinition (SAMR) model, which is a way of analyzing how much impact technology has on your teaching, technology is categorized on a spectrum that ranges from substitution to redefinition. Substitution occurs when you teach the same way with or without tech (taking notes on a paper or taking notes on a tablet). Redefinition happens when you use technology to teach in ways that would be impossible without the tech, like students working on a project collaboratively with students in another country. SAMR is a great model and is useful for incorporating technology in learning, but it is very theoretical. I (Matt) have worked to explain the SAMR model to teachers in learning, but the more I talked about the model and the theory, the more their eyes glazed over. The differences seem subtle, and the explanation can sound confusing. But when I connect the different stages of SAMR to actual practices in the classroom, suddenly it clicks with these new teachers—and they can see how they might use technology in more meaningful ways with their students.

Ditching habits in the pursuit of eventually ditching homework comes down to making changes in our classroom that cause learning to really *stick*. Teachers and students have long studied and worked at learning in hopes that their efforts weren't in vain. They hoped that if they worked hard enough and studied long enough, the new ideas and information would stick.

Instead of going by "what we've always done" or "what seems to make sense," as teachers, we can encourage students to rely on learning methods that are proven by cognitive science. More importantly, we can model these strategies in our own lives. Students will take their cue from us when they see how practicing spaced retrieval, developing positive habits, and increasing physical activity help make learning stick —without the need for homework. And that's when we have our best chance of setting them on a course for future success.

CHAPTER 6
DITCH THAT REMEDIATION

> HELPING STUDENTS
> PREPARE FOR COLLEGE
> AND THE REAL WORLD

MANY SAY THE GOAL OF K-12 EDUCATION IS TO PREPARE STUDENTS FOR LIFE AFTER GRADUATION. If that's true, one of the first milestones to life in the "real world" is graduation. Seventeen percent of public high school students drop out of school, according to the National Center for Education Statistics (*DitchThatHomework.com/HSdropout*). College dropout rates aren't much better. The six-year graduation rate for first-time, full-time undergraduate students pursuing a bachelor's degree was 60 percent in 2008 (*DitchThatHomework.com/collegedropout*). As educators, two of our main priorities are to encourage kids to stay in school and to equip them with the skills they need to succeed—in school and in life.

Some old-school educators argue that homework helps prepare students for life after school because it teaches responsibility. But does it really? We hope that if you've gotten this far in the book, you understand that homework is not as effective or valuable a tool as we've been led to believe. In fact, homework can squelch a student's love for learning and, for some, may even drive them away from considering higher education.

As an adjunct professor, I (Alice) can tell you, from experience, that homework in college is no more well received or useful than it is at earlier grade levels. Having been saddled with homework in high school doesn't make kids excited or even prepared for homework in college. What *does* prepare students for life after graduation? More importantly, what prepares them to finish high school so they have the opportunity to pursue college or a lucrative trade? Real-life skills that they can use today—and tomorrow.

> "As a parent, I teach important life lessons not in the school curriculum. Home is not just another school period."
>
> —JOHN MILLER, PARENT AND TEACHER

> "I didn't do much homework in high school and have maintained straight A's throughout college."
>
> —DENISE VON MINDEN, SCHOOL LIBRARIAN

POSSIBLE GROUP PROJECT ROLES

 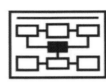

Editor	Organizer	Recorder
Leader	Marketer	Presenter
Researcher	Graphic Designer	Fact Checker

Icons: Gregor Cresnar, Gan Khoon Lay, erikTS, Aleksandr Vector, Arafat Uddin, OB via TheNounProject.com

We all know successful college graduates who did not do much homework in high school. As an adjunct faculty member at a university, I (Alice) see that successful college students do more than remain compliant in completing assignments to succeed. If we get real, what variables can we control that will help students be successful in college?

In this chapter, we'll address eight key skills that can really affect how much students *thrive* (rather than survive homework). This chapter is longer than others, but that's done on purpose. We want to dive into the skills that can really affect students' success beyond school.

1. Solid Study Skills

Assigning something does not teach it. Similarly, telling students to go home and study does not teach them study skills. Some students have well-educated, invested parents at home who help them practice smart study skills. That's great for those kids, but if you're leaving it to the parents to help students figure out how to develop study skills, some of your students will most certainly suffer academically. To ensure all of your students have the study skills they need to succeed, now and in college, build in time for practicing those skills in the classroom.

> "Study skills, not homework, prepare for college. Homework doesn't automatically create study skills."
>
> —Rachel Stearns, middle school language arts teacher

A British psychological study found a college success indicator: college grade point average combined with the students' beliefs in themselves to perform (performance self-efficacy) (Richardson et al. 2012). Among its findings was that grade-point average correlated with self-efficacy. Students who believed in themselves had better grades. This is something we can help with in the K-12 world. Helping students feel confident about themselves as learners prepares them for college. Even if students reach the college level without high self-efficacy, it's not too late. Research has found that study skills and study skill courses are significant in student success in college (Wernersbach et al. 2014).

> "Leverage technology to spend more time working with students in small groups to develop specific skills."
>
> —CATLIN TUCKER, ENGLISH TEACHER AND AUTHOR,
> *BLENDED LEARNING IN ACTION*

Giving students both choice and decision-making power is crucial to helping them learn how to study. When students find their best method of studying, they can enter the college environment with confidence. As a teacher, you can help by offering students study choices, reviewing their choices with them, and providing guidance on how they can improve their study techniques.

Here are some study-skill choices that educators in all roles can encourage students to try:

When taking notes, synthesize instead of copying. Recording information improves retention, but copying information is a low cognitive skill. Mindlessly copying material does little to nothing to help the brain to remember what has been taught. To improve the learning experience and retention, encourage students to synthesize the information they're taking in, making decisions about what's important and what's not before writing it down in notes.

DITCH THAT HOMEWORK RESOURCES

Try a collaborative notetaking activity to allow students to pool their efforts on finding resources and logging what they're learning. A collaborative spreadsheet in Google Sheets can allow for each student to have his or her own tab, with his or her name on it, in a spreadsheet to organize what he or she finds.

Try the Google Sheets TemplateTab Add-on to create a collaborative resource for students to contribute to. Paste a roster of student names on the first sheet. Design a graphic organizer if desired on the second sheet. A tab for each student will be created with a copy of the graphic organizer. Share the spreadsheet with editing access for all students.

TemplateTab Template:
ditchthathomework.com/templatetab

Encourage good reading strategies. Reading academic texts is different than reading a magazine. Rather than just assigning a reading, include specific strategies for students to employ in order to tackle the text. Surprisingly, some techniques we may think are helping students can have negligible or negative impacts on learning. For example, having students underline a text can have a negative effect when used as a study technique (Peterson 1991). Good reading strategies include having students identify unfamiliar vocabulary, connecting content to prior experiences, interacting with other readers, skimming and rereading, identifying a main idea, and looking for textual features. Peter Afflerbach, a professor who specializes in reading strategies, suggests having students ask themselves, "Does that make sense?" after each sentence (Afflerbach 2008).

Create test questions. Rather than filling out a study guide, students can create their own test questions. Students may enjoy making test questions in game-based review sites like Kahoot!, Quizizz, Quia, or another digital platform. Formulating questions helps them see the material from another vantage point—the teacher's—and encourages ownership of learning.

Create with what you're learning. When students engage with the content, they are more likely to remember it. What can students do with the information beyond creating flashcards? How do they personalize the information and make it their own? In Chapter 1, we offered a few ideas, including blogs, websites, and videos. Creating content that is intended to be shared with an authentic audience forces students to synthesize the material and put it into their own words, a process that boosts retention.

Engage in a discussion board. In a face-to-face discussion, a limited number of students get to do the talking, which means the rest of the students may be tuning out. Digital discussion options allow all students to voice their thoughts and questions on the content or topic.

Encourage students to go to bed. Staying up late to cram for a test is counter-productive. Study skills go beyond using flashcards and drinking a lot of coffee. A good night of sleep and a good breakfast can be a student's best friends when it comes to clarity of thought and recall ability.

DITCH THAT HOMEWORK RESOURCES

Try one of these digital discussion board options:

- Google Classroom Create a Question feature (classroom.google.com)
- Schoology discussion board (schoology.com)
- TodaysMeet (todaysmeet.com)
- InsertLearning (insertlearning.com)
- Padlet (padlet.com)

---

2. DECISION-MAKING AND INDEPENDENT LEARNING SKILLS

In college, students make countless decisions every day. That means that *before* they get to college, they need to practice making decisions and learn to think for themselves. Following teacher directions and doing compliance-based activities don't help students become independent learners. When designing lessons, consider how students can take ownership of their learning. Offer opportunities that encourage students to make choices rather than simply follow directions.

> "Spoon feeding, in the long run, teaches us nothing but the shape of the spoon."
>
> —E.M. FORSTER, ENGLISH NOVELIST

THE SUCCEED MODEL

(S) ## SELECT TOPIC
Students choose topic and identify what information they need.

(U) ## UNCOVER SOURCES 🔍
Students find potential sources of information and learn how to access them.

(C) ## COLLECT RESOURCES
Students collect resources they may need and examine them. Then, they determine which ones are suitable.

(C) ## COMPILE RELEVANT INFO
From the resources they've collected, students determine what information is relevant.

(E) ## EVALUATE INFORMATION
Students evaluate, interpret, analyze and synthesize information, creating a cohesive message.

(E) ## ESTABLISH PRESENTATION
Students choose a format to clearly communicate their ideas and the information.

(D) ## DETERMINE EFFECTIVENESS
Students reflect on their learning and their process. How effective were they?

Icons: Kirill Ulitin, i cons, Aleksandr Vector, TooJooGoo, OCHA Visual Information Unit, Gregor Cresnar, Michael V. Suriano, B. Farias via TheNounProject.com

DITCH **THAT HOMEWORK**

Robert Barr and John Tagg of Palomar College in San Marcos, California, write that educational institutions should be focused on learning outcomes instead of teaching or instructing (Barr and Tagg 1995). Think about that. Teaching or instructing is a top-down approach. It's something that's done *to* someone. Learning is something that anyone can own and wield to their advantage. Empowering students to learn helps create independent learners.

Consider providing students a challenge connected to a learning objective rather than a preset task. Suzanne DeLong, in work with the U.S. Military Academy's Center for Faculty Excellence, suggests to help students connect learning with their abilities, needs, and interests. Likewise, encourage them to identify what they value and how they best learn. Then, facilitate assessments in conjunction with student self-assessments (DeLong 2009). When students become accustomed to self-assessment, they're using skills to independently guide their own learning—the skills they'll depend on when they leave school.

DeLong (2009) offers a list of activities that can encourage independent learners:

- Collaborative instructional techniques
- Students research, receive feedback, and reflect
- Blended learning
- Virtual field trips
- Active learning activities such as debates, role playing, simulations, peer teaching, and in-class writing
- Interactive lectures
- Small group discussions
- Project work

- Problem-based learning

- Students choose their own topics

DITCH THAT HOMEWORK RESOURCES

In some classes, even those where the teacher tries to innovate as much as possible, research papers are still a way of life. To help students organize their resources for a paper, try the Note Taker add-on for Google Docs that I (Alice) created. Students collect and organize their notes on the spreadsheet. After selecting the order in which they wish their notes to appear, a rough draft is created and pushed to a Google Doc for students to evaluate and edit.

Add-on Template:
ditchthathomework.com/notetaker

3. CRITICAL THINKING SKILLS

Sometimes, it's hard to know what kinds of assignments really challenge students to think critically at high levels. For example, math problems like the one below are literally made into cartoons because they seem so difficult:

A train leaves the station at 40 mph headed east at 2:15 p.m. Three hours later, another train leaves the station headed west at 35 mph. At what time are they 300 miles apart?

Even though most people would say this is a hard question to solve, procedurally it is not very complex. There are concrete steps to follow that will yield the correct answer. It's a paint-by-numbers problem when what we'd really like is a well-thought-out masterpiece.

Because critical thinking is a necessary skill for college (and non-college career paths), increasing the critical-thinking level of assignments is essential. As a math teacher, when I (Alice) started to evaluate the critical-thinking skills required by the textbook, I realized that almost the entire algebra book was level 1 on Webb's Depth of Knowledge (DOK) scale with some DOK level 2. My fellow teachers and I thought we were teaching students to think, but in reality, we were working with low-level critical-thinking tasks.

Webb's Depth of Knowledge is a scale of 1 to 4. It's like a Bloom's Taxonomy for critical thinking (More information: *ditchthathomework.com/dok*). Usually worksheets are about finding an answer and following directions. These are DOK 1 tasks; they're about following steps—something that some students can do without much original thought. Webb's Depth of Knowledge doesn't look at how hard a task is (with a complicated list of tasks) but rather its *complexity.* (With so many factors, success isn't a given.)

In my own unscientific surveys, I ask students, "What percent of work that you do in school is busywork?" Students never respond with a low number. Typical responses are 75 or 85 percent. There's a disconnect between what students and teachers perceive as meaningful work. I know very few educators who would label their assignments as busywork. So why do teacher and student perceptions vary so greatly?

Like the problems in the algebra textbook I mentioned, too many homework assignments focus on DOK 1 and DOK 2 tasks. Students are asked to memorize, recall, or follow directions. It's pretty easy to see how students could see that kind of activity as busywork. A better option for developing critical thinking skills is to give them the opportunity to do more DOK 3 and even DOK 4 work. When possible, ask them to summarize materials, use context clues, explain their thought process, and make and refute claims.

DEPTH OF KNOWLEDGE (DOK)

IT IS ABOUT CRITICAL THINKING! NOT VERBS!

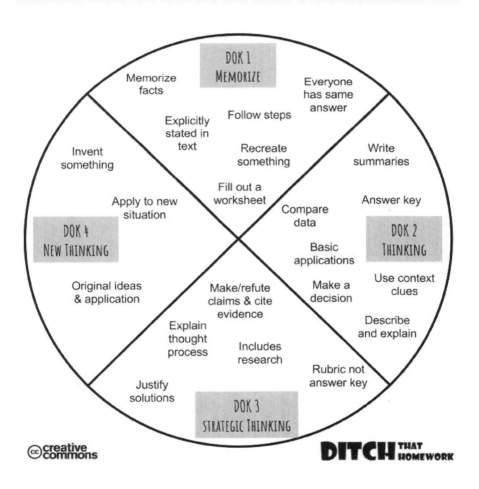

DITCH THAT HOMEWORK

Rigor does not equate to quantity. Giving students more work to do at home does not increase the rigor of a course. DOK 3 is defined by strategic thinking. Providing more opportunities for students to engage in strategic thinking will increase the rigor of the course and better prepare students simply because they are developing their critical thinking skills.

> "When choosing EdTech, we need to consider DOK for students. If it is teacher-focused and only level 1, use sparingly."
>
> —SHANNON DOAK, TECHNOLOGY COACH

You can't talk kids into being critical thinkers. You have to give them a chance to think, receive feedback, and then to reflect and think some more. If you want assignments to reflect that kind of deep thinking, design them to be "back-and-forth assignments" rather than "one-and-done assignments." Completing work and receiving a grade doesn't do as much to encourage critical thinking as does reflecting and responding to feedback. And the best time to give feedback is during the learning process, not after. For many students, as soon as they receive a grade for their work, they see learning as done.

> GIVING STUDENTS MORE WORK TO DO AT HOME DOES NOT INCREASE THE RIGOR OF A COURSE.

Shift from "answer the question" to "identify and solve a problem."

Shift from "show your steps" to "explain your thinking."

 Ask "What would happen if …"

HOW TO KICK DEPTH OF KNOWLEDGE UP A NOTCH

 Identify a problem and provide a solution.

 Create a for/against argument with evidence.

Ask open-ended questions that do not have one answer (even better if there is NO answer)!

Ask questions that ask students to make a claim and justify it.

 Value multiple approaches to solving a problem.

Respond to the prompt with a unique solution.

Compare and contrast solutions.

DITCH THAT HOMEWORK

Completed. Finished. Time to move on to something else. Offering feedback throughout the learning process helps ensure that students will read the feedback (not just toss it in the trash) and use it to rethink, revise, and improve their work.

DITCH THAT HOMEWORK RESOURCES

Making mistakes and devising new strategies is part of the learning process. Help students see beyond the value of "getting the answer" by asking them to document and reflect on the learning process.

If students are using digital tools, they can take screenshots periodically to capture their attempts, successes, and failures. If students are doing projects and building things, they can take pictures with a mobile device or use a portable camera such as the iPevo (goo.gl/ChrcMQ) to capture the process. Students can use a variety of digital presentation options to organize reflections on their learning.

Storybird.com	Sway.com
Storyboardthat.com	iMovie
Animoto.com	Wevideo.com
Prezi.com	Movenote.com
Piktochart.com	Adobe Spark
Sites.google.com	

Presentation software such as Google Slides can also be an excellent platform to allow students to show their thinking. Collaborative tools, such as Google Slides, allow the teacher to insert feedback conversations to help the students to develop their thinking.

The Alice Keeler SlideShot Chrome extension automatically takes a screenshot each minute and saves it to Google Drive. Students can also manually add screenshots using the extension. Upon clicking "Finish," a Google Slides presentation is automatically created with each of the screenshots along with a text box for students to reflect on their process.

Chrome Extension:
ditchthathomework.com/slideshot

When you make the shift to higher critical thinking tasks, expect resistance. Complex thinking is hard work! For many students, it's new territory. Following the teacher's directions is much easier than coming up with your own ideas. A student who asks you, "Can't you just give me a worksheet or quiz instead?" is really asking you to do the hard work of thinking *for* them.

Resistance to critical thinking often manifests itself in incomplete work that turns into homework. When talking about homework with teachers, Matt and I often hear things like, "It is only homework if they did not finish it in class." But when I've asked my own child, "Why didn't you finish this in class?" the answer is, "I didn't understand it."

When students choose to finish an assignment at home, it's a procrastination tactic. They're delaying cognitively taxing work because, let's face it, it is uncomfortable. If they say they're going to do it at home, what they're really saying is that they want a break—or to just stop doing the work.

If a student is struggling on an assignment, sending them home to struggle—often for an excessive amount of time—doesn't help. Parents may try to intervene if they have the time and ability to help. In fact, I (Alice) have heard from parents who have done assignments for their kids because they thought the struggling required was excessive. The fact that the student is already struggling makes the situation ripe for stress and conflict.

Jon Corippo, chief innovation officer for CUE (*cue.org*), points out that if students are not using their time well in class, we shouldn't reward procrastination tactics by letting them do the work at home. Given the option, students prefer spending time socializing with friends than being on task. Don't give them that option. Instead, provide guidance in class and adjust the task to the student. A more student-centered classroom allows teachers more time to sit and help students one-on-one when they struggle.

Students will eventually come around and discover personal satisfaction in developing their own thinking abilities. It's like Plato's cave allegory; When students come out of a dark cave, the sunlight hurts their eyes. It seems easier and less painful for them to turn around and go back into the cave. Many students (and adults) are looking for the path of least resistance. To help them succeed—to really prepare them for life after graduation—we must persist, provide support and encouragement, and resist the urge to give in and give them a worksheet. Their eyes will eventually adjust to the sunlight and they'll see a whole new realm.

4. Digital Research Skills

It is essential for students to be good researchers of information. Teaching is not talking but rather designing the learning environment

> TEACHING IS NOT TALKING
> BUT RATHER DESIGNING THE
> LEARNING ENVIRONMENT
> AND ENGAGING STUDENTS.

and engaging students. If we teach students research skills, they will be able to answer open-ended, high-level critical thinking questions.

Research today is *totally* different than when we were students. We used to start by creating a thesis statement and identifying key ideas. We created outlines to frame our research. Then, we hit the library. We gathered resources from encyclopedias (yes, the ones made of paper, not Wikipedia!). We used the card catalog to find books. We browsed magazines, newspapers, and journals.

Few of today's students will ever touch a physical encyclopedia or open a paper dictionary—except to say, "Whoa, did you guys *really* use these?!" They will, however, almost assuredly use digital resources. As digital natives, today's students consider tech resources non-negotiable (along with WiFi).

It's a cultural norm to use Google to look things up, and knowing how to do digital research is a vital skill for work and life. Here are a few ways to help students cultivate strong research skills in the Internet age.

First, help students understand that copying and pasting off the Internet is plagiarism. Understanding fair use, public domain, and Creative Commons is a good place to start. These are resources licensed for use by anyone (provided that they abide by certain stipulations).

A common misconception is that students can use whatever they want from the Internet as long as they give credit to the source. If students publish their copied work on a blog or website, they may well receive a take-down letter from someone's lawyer. We can help students exercise digital citizenship by understanding and abiding by licenses of creative works. Digital does not necessarily equal free, and credit is not the same as permission.

Second, teach students that searching keywords is different from typing in a question. Ask Jeeves was a search engine in the 1990s that became popular because it would answer your questions. Really, it was just a smarter search engine that did the same thing other search engines do today: Seek out words on a page.

Sadly, our search habits haven't evolved much since the 1990s. Ask students to do some Internet research and many will just type the question you asked into Google. It helps to understand that the search is looking for specific words, keywords, on the page—not answering the question.

Understanding how to use keywords effectively will empower students to do better research—and better work. For instance, word order is important (most important words should be listed first in a search), as are plurality (how often words are found on a page), quotations, and synonyms. See the infographic to the right for some suggestions.

Each word in a search plays a crucial role. For example, a search for "dog research" won't get great results because the article you want probably does not contain the word research. Instead of using the word "research," students can use a subtopic to narrow the results they find, like "Labrador Retriever origin." The key here is that the word *research* doesn't add to the keyword search. Have students think about the words and phrases that might actually be on the page they are hoping to find. To narrow the search to research articles, students

KEYWORD TIPS

(1) IDENTIFY KEYWORDS

Don't ask a question; think of words associated with your topic.

Topic: What increases student motivation when using digital resources?

Keywords: student, motivation, digital, online, resources

(2) BRAINSTORM ALTERNATIVES

What other words might the author have used besides your keyword?

Motivation: motivate, motivates, motivating, encourages

(3) USE QUOTATIONS 🙾

Use quotation marks to find the phrase exactly as typed.

Student Motivation vs. "Student Motivation"

(4) USE BOOLEAN OPERATORS 🔍

Using AND and OR helps narrow a search. The asterisk wildcard finds anything that has the part you typed.

Ex: Student AND Motiv*

(5) EXCLUDE ⊖

Exclude keywords with a minus or NOT

Ex: "Digital Resources" -PowerPoint

Icons: Gregor Cresnar, iconsphere, Deepz, Aleks via TheNounProject.com

DITCH THAT HOMEWORK

should consider the source where the desired information might be located and restrict their search to sites that end in EDU by using "site:.edu" in the address bar in an advanced search. Students can also use Google Scholar (*scholar.google.com*) to restrict their search to research articles.

A keyword search is likely to call up millions of possible results. Students need to know that the top results are not necessarily the best resources. Organizations pay money to appear higher in the search results. They intentionally design their websites to rank higher in Internet searches. Showing up first in an Internet search doesn't equate to having the best quality content.

Try this activity with students to improve their searching savvy: Have them do a search on a topic related to class. Without clicking on anything, have students analyze the results in front of them and justify which ones are most likely to have the best content and why.

Third, help students learn how to analyze a URL. A common misconception is that a *"dot org"* site is more reliable. False! Anyone can buy a *"dot org"* website. What comes after the dot often doesn't indicate reliability or expertise. Exceptions: Some domain extensions—the part after the dot—are regulated. Examples include .edu, .gov, and .mil. The content on these sites is not regulated. For example, college students can often get their own web pages through .edu sites and post whatever they want. Also, government agencies can change the content on government websites to reflect the politics of those in power.

DITCH THAT HOMEWORK RESOURCES

Keyboard shortcuts can save students time and improve their research experience. Here are a few tips:

- A quick keyboard shortcut tip to help students be savvy searchers is to hold down the Control key (Windows/Chromebook) or Command key (Mac) when clicking a link to open it in another tab. This keeps the tab with the original search intact so they can go back to it. When they're done with the new tab, they can close it to return to the original search.

- Another helpful keyboard shortcut is CTRL-W (Windows/Chromebook) or Command-W (Mac). This closes a web page quickly if it doesn't contain the right information or if it's redundant. Using CTRL-W / Command-W saves time and effort in small doses, which really adds up over time.

- The keyboard shortcut CTRL-F (Windows/Chromebook) or Command-F (Mac) can also help with finding relevant information. CTRL-F/Command-F opens a pop-up window in which they can insert a specific word or phrase on the page. Each occurrence of the word or phrase will then be highlighted on the screen. Students can look at each occurrence of the keyword(s) and the surrounding context to determine if the site potentially has information they want to use.

Fourth, help students become better skimmers. Skimming is a crucial skill in our information-heavy world. With the billions of pages on the Internet, it's a time-saver to know how to quickly scan a page to determine whether it's worth your time. For younger students, in particular, skimming isn't intuitive. Let's teach this skill explicitly to students.

Finally, teach students to analyze the credibility of online sources. Many students have a misconception that anything on the Internet is true. The 2016 presidential election really brought to light the idea of "fake news." It is incredibly easy to publish and widely distribute untruths. It was once possible to "triangulate" information—find it in three separate places—to prove it was true. Not so anymore. False information spreads like wildfire on the Internet and is copied and pasted into multiple sites. It can be very tricky to determine if a source is valid. Here are some questions for students to thoughtfully consider the credibility of a source:

- Who is the author?
- Who sponsored the site?
- Is the spelling and grammar up to par?
- Is it a *.edu* site? Is it a *.gov* site?
- Is the site a blog or a wiki?
- What reason would the author have to have bias?
- What are other points of view?
- Are there advertisements on the site?
- What is the quality of the web design?
- Breaking down the URL, does it appear credible?

Catlin Tucker created the "Got Credibility" form, which she hosts on her blog for teachers and students to access (*DitchThatHomework. com/gotcredibility*). The form walks users through several questions to evaluate websites. It asks about the author's credibility, the organization associated with the author, bias found in the article, whether it has current information, and misspellings/grammatical errors, among other things.

For older students, learning to use Google Scholar (*scholar.google. com*) and the library's database resources will help them be successful in college. Partner with your school librarian to ensure that students leave your class with the ability to locate and take full advantage of academic resources through the library and online databases.

5. The Skill of Meeting Authentic Deadlines

For most people, deadlines are flexible, at least to a degree. Benjamin Franklin said, "In this world nothing can be said to be certain, except death and taxes," but even taxes aren't hard and fast in their deadlines. The April 15th filing date for federal income tax may be the most widely recognized hard deadline we have in the United States. Even though everyone is aware of that date, we also know that extensions can be granted.

Except in rare circumstances, in our everyday lives, we do not have to submit something every day. So when we assign a due date to students, we have to ask ourselves *why* we're setting a specific date as a deadline. Is it arbitrary, or is there an authentic reason for the due date?

When possible, let's find some authentic deadlines. When students present to an audience, the deadline is authentic. They must be ready while the audience is there. If students are tasked with a project like creating pamphlets distributed at a community fair, the deadline is authentic. They must finish the pamphlets before people arrive. Identify a few due dates throughout the year for which students can plan in advance.

6. TEAMWORK SKILLS

While the idea of group work may elicit a groan from many students, the solution is not to avoid this type of work. Being a part of a group and following through on parts of the project teach students responsibility.

It is unrealistic and unnecessary for each student to do equal work in a group. Think of the groups we're involved in through our real lives: teacher work groups, community service groups, church activity groups, etc. Does everyone really do the same amount of work? Of course not, nor are they expected to. I have been involved in zero group activities, academically, personally or professionally where every member was an equal contributor.

When assigning group projects, ask students to take inventory of each person's unique talents and decide how those talents can be used to positively reach the end goal. Students can identify their roles, plan how they'll use their time, and specify the tasks they are responsible for. Then, they can create a deadline and start assigning tasks to meet milestones.

Each student can design a rubric for his/her involvement based on the plans the group created. At the end of the project, ask students to self-assess using their own rubric *and* assess each fellow group member.

SKILLS OF THE FUTURE

(1) PROBLEM SOLVING

Following directions is what robots do. Knowing how to identify, analyze and solve a complex problem is a timeless skill.

(2) CREATIVITY

Now that information is at our fingertips, there's power in being able to create something useful out of it.

(3) PEOPLE MANAGEMENT

As the world changes quickly, one skill that won't vanish is the ability to work with and lead others.

(4) EMOTIONAL INTELLIGENCE

In interpersonal work, it's vital to be able to read, recognize and react to others' emotions and feelings.

(5) MAKING JUDGMENTS

We make hundreds of decisions every day. Using sound reasoning and logic can improve our work and our lives.

Icons: Gregor Cresnar, Brandon Shields via TheNounProject.com

DITCH THAT HOMEWORK

Self and peer assessment has many benefits. First, students take the responsibility of assessment off the teacher's plate and share that responsibility with each other. Second, self-reflection helps students take ownership of their work. This is important because learning to critically evaluate one's own work is an important skill that students will need when they enter the workforce. A study in Scotland by David J. Nicol and Debra Macfarlane-Dick explains that when teachers do all of the assessment and feedback, students don't develop these important self-regulation and self-evaluation skills (Nicol and Macfarlane-Dick 2006).

7. Short-Term Goal-Setting Skills

How students feel about themselves academically matters. Their belief in their ability to succeed (self-efficacy) has a large impact on student success, according to *Academic Tenacity: Mindsets and Skills that Promote Long-Term Learning* (Dweck et al. 2011). Students with lower self-efficacy struggle to believe their efforts will lead to success. Low scores, being wrong, or formative feedback can cast a negative tone and often reinforce students' beliefs that they are not capable. They can turn to coping techniques, like withdrawing and simply not trying. These are defense mechanisms students employ. They believe that they are not dumb if they just don't try.

When given homework, students with higher self-efficacy are more likely to complete it because they feel more confident that their efforts will lead to success. If students think they won't be successful, they are less likely to complete the homework. That puts struggling students at a disadvantage, which is something I can't stand for.

I (Alice) noticed this with my students. The ones who didn't need the practice were the ones who did the homework, but the ones who really needed it didn't. This created two negative situations: It created busywork for my higher achievers who already got it, and it wasn't helping my lower achievers since they weren't going to do the homework regardless. Cancelling homework for my high school math classes allowed me to think differently about how I design my in-class time to support my struggling students. Success builds success. Helping them to find success led to more positive attitudes about learning math.

So how can we help students to build that crucial self-efficacy? By setting short-term goals. Stanford researcher and *Mindsets* author, Carol Dweck, speaks often about growth mindset as well as goal-setting. In one research study, Dweck and fellow researcher Elaine Elliott found that goal-setting contributes to motivation and achievement (Dweck and Elliott 1988). Setting and achieving short-term goals help students to achieve long-term goals. It's like that old saying: *"How do you eat an elephant? One bite at a time."*

Again in *Academic Tenacity*, Dweck, Walton, and Cohen found that students need to set a specific goal and have a concrete plan of how to accomplish it (Dweck et al. 2011). *"I will get a B"* is not a good short-term goal. It's too vague and the path to accomplishing it is unclear. It's like when we travel; we need a roadmap or GPS with turn-by-turn directions. We can't just decide we're going to travel to San Francisco and jump in the car with no clear route to get there.

In the same way, students need to learn how to identify specific steps to take. By setting short-term goals to complete each step, they begin to see that their goals are achievable—and that's empowering. Instead of saying, "I will get a B," a better goal would be to find ten sources by Friday to support their topic idea. That's a very clear first step to a good grade on a project.

We (students *and* educators) can use this step-by-step approach to setting any short-term goal. Start by identifying the goal. Write down the goal and identify the steps to achieving it. Later, follow up on the goals and reflect on why the goal was achieved (or why it wasn't achieved). When we become better goal-setters, we become better self-regulators of our own learning. Isn't that the goal?

DITCH THAT HOMEWORK RESOURCES

Digitally collecting short-term goals can help record the goal-setting conversations and connect the feedback. The key is not just to collect the goals but to review them and follow up with students.

Using Google Classroom, create an assignment where students identify their goal in the private comments of the assignment. This allows for the teacher to efficiently reply to students to help them develop their goal. At the end of the week, students can come back to the assignment and reflect on their achievement of the goal in the private comments.

Google Forms is an excellent tool for collecting data. Send the data collected to a Google Sheets spreadsheet where you can sort and filter the goals. Try using a pivot table in the spreadsheet to summarize the data collected. Add-ons for Google Sheets that may be helpful include Autocrat to generate a report for each student after submitting their goals or the RowCall Add-on to segregate each student's weekly submissions into their own sheet.

Weekly Short-Term Goal-Setting Google Form:
DitchThatHomework.com/goals

8. Informal Learning Skills

Informal learning is some of the best learning there is. It's directed by the learner and is *"just in time"* learning—learning on demand in the moment when the learner needs it—instead of *"just in case"* learning. Research by Julian Sefton-Green of Wac Performing Arts and Media College states that digital-age students naturally engage in informal learning by looking up information on YouTube or the Internet and posting it on their own websites or YouTube channels to share their learning (Sefton-Green 2004).

Sometimes, informal learning is viewed as time wasting—like cruising YouTube and social media to kill time. But this kind of learning is nothing to scoff at. As adults, we practice informal learning on an almost daily basis. Need to know how to fix a leaky pipe? There's a YouTube video for that. Want to know why your computer is running so slowly? You'll find lots of fix-it tutorial articles online.

When students are not assigned formal learning (i.e., homework) to do outside of class, they are able to explore things they are passionate about. We see this when students come to school so excited to share something new they learned. It is amazing what kids will do and come up with when they have the time. When students are inspired by what they learn in class, many will explore the topic further and extend their learning outside of class—by choice.

Just because we (as adults and teachers) may not see the value of topics that students pursue outside of class doesn't mean they aren't valuable. What's *most* valuable, though, is helping students discover and pursue their passions outside of class as a means of becoming better humans. For example, if you have a Minecraft fan in your class, help him see how the game promotes his ability to conceive and prototype new ideas. Or if you have a committed athlete in your class, help her see how she's developing persistence and perseverance through practice.

Extracurricular activities are awesome examples of informal learning, and robotics clubs are a perfect example. Robotics engineering develops problem-solving and STEM skills. As students work together, they build confidence, learn teamwork skills, and practice researching and exploring. If students are burdened with hours of homework, this kind of passion-producing, student-owned learning isn't possible.

Have students share what they are learning outside of class—and celebrate it. Consider finding ways to give students credit for their informal learning. Do students only earn points by completing teacher-directed tasks? If students can find their own way to show what they know *and* receive credit, their motivation to extend their learning increases. In short, value learning over compliance. If you are not using a standards-based gradebook, consider inserting the learning objective into the gradebook rather than the assignment. Doing so provides more opportunities for differentiation and for students to show their learning in various ways.

"Nobody ever thinks back to school and remembers 'that really awesome worksheet.' They remember experiences, presenting, field trips, and other things that were engaging. No one ever thinks about a worksheet again."

—Karen Mensing, first and second grade teacher

As teachers, as parents, and as people in general, we want to help students prepare for the future. We want them to succeed in college and in the workplace—whatever that may look like for them.

Well-meaning teachers assign homework thinking that they're preparing students for the future by doing it, but research and best practice just don't support homework as a viable means of college preparation. Our experiences (Alice and Matt) and those of teachers, parents, and others we've encountered don't back up the use of homework either. We can (and should!) ditch homework and teach these crucial eight skills that will serve our students beyond graduation. If we want to help develop well-rounded human beings, higher quality assignments are a step in the right direction.

CHAPTER 7
DITCH THAT COMPLIANCE

> ### HELPING STUDENTS OWN
> ### THEIR LEARNING

THE GOAL OF SCHOOL IS LEARNING. I (Alice) didn't get into teaching so I could distribute points. I'm betting that you didn't either. If you're anything like me, you became a teacher because you wanted to make a difference in kids' lives, something that starts by helping them learn—about themselves and the world around them.

I truly believe that students would rather learn than eat. But they often get discouraged when the work they're doing is perceived to be about compliance—mindlessly following teacher directions that don't seem to have bearing on their lives—rather than authentic learning.

Looking ahead to the skills our students will need in their future, ingenuity and learning skills will be far more important than being able to follow directions. Employers will be looking for innovators, self-starters and problem solvers. Because today, almost anything that involves following procedural steps can be automated, even something seemingly complex as driving a car.

Our quest as educators isn't to teach kids how to follow directions. That won't prepare students to thrive in the marketplace. Our mission is to equip and inspire kids to become lifelong learners.

> "Our school culture is such that we reward completion and compliance on homework. This practice strengthens the gap between the 'have and have not' students."
>
> —NICK SCHUMACHER, SCHOOL ADMINISTRATOR

In *Ditch That Textbook*, Matt compares some students to the people who used to rent a house he owned. They paid the rent because they had to. They lived in the house, but they didn't make any improvements to it. They were renters. They had no vested interest in making the house the best it could be.

Students can easily take this approach to learning. If they aren't investing in it in meaningful ways, they're metaphorically paying rent and getting by month by month. They're *complying* so that they don't get in trouble for poor grades or bad behavior—the "live to fight another day" mindset. The key question educators must answer is, *how do we get the renters to sign the deed and become owners? How do we help motivate students to own their education?*

Here's a hint: Compliance-based homework assignments aren't going to do it. Ownership of learning happens when students get excited about directing their own learning and, in turn, directing their own lives.

HELP STUDENTS LEARN RESPONSIBILITY

Many parents take up the homework fight, believing that it teaches responsibility. However, Lyn Corno, in a research article in *Educational Researcher*, writes, "There is almost no evidence that homework fosters discipline and personal responsibility." When parents push for homework to teach responsibility, they really seem to be saying this: "If I had to endure it, you have to, too" (Corno 1996). We can just let the "responsibility" myth die. Too often, the person who is responsible for everything in the classroom is the teacher. If we want to teach students responsibility, we have to give them real responsibilities.

Catlin Tucker, author of the book *Blended Learning in Action*, offers this insight on her blog (*DitchThatHomework.com/tuckerwork*):

Who does the following tasks in your classroom:

- *Plans daily lessons*
- *Teaches or facilitates each lesson*
- *Designs projects*
- *Troubleshoots technology hiccups*
- *Assesses student work*
- *Communicates with parents about student progress*

If the answer to most of these questions is you, the teacher, then you've already realized you are doing the lion's share of the work in your classroom. Of course, the teacher's role in designing curriculum and establishing norms is key, especially at the beginning of the year. But I think teachers, in

TEACH RESPONSIBILITY

(1) ASSIGN CLASS JOBS

Consider naming student jobs with authentic job titles: IT Support, Engineer, Designer, Office Manager, etc.*

(2) STUDENT AGENCY

How can we empower students to make their own decisions about learning throughout the day?

(3) ACCOUNTABILITY

Is a student's work dependent upon the work of others? Do they realize how their actions impact others?

(4) PLAN A LESSON

Are students doing activities or designing activities? Are they leading other students?

(5) AUTHENTIC DUE DATES

How are your due dates determined? Are they arbitrary, or are they based on an actual, immovable deadline?

(6) REFLECTION

Let kids make decisions and fail sometimes. When things don't work, don't give detention. Instead, let's think about it.

Source: http://www.westpoint.edu/cfe/Literature/ DeLongS_09.pdf. Job names idea via Tana Raiyne (Twitter: @TanaRaiyne). Icons: Chameleon Design, mikicon, Gregor Cresnar, Ralf Schmitzer, ArtWorkLeaf via TheNounProject.com

DITCH THAT HOMEWORK

general, try to do too much and don't expect their students to do enough (Tucker 2016).

Peter Pappas, a college professor in Portland, Oregon, echoes Tucker's sentiments. In a post to his *"Copy / Paste"* blog (*DitchThatHomework.com/pappas*), he says:

> We need to craft learning environments that ask students to increasingly take responsibility for their learning—products, process, and evaluation.
>
> Unfortunately, most of our students get a steady diet of force-fed information and test-taking strategies. We're giving a generation of kids practice for predictable, routine procedures—and that happens across the "bell curve" from AP test prep to meeting minimal proficiency on NCLB-mandated tests (Pappas 2011).

Students need the responsibility of making decisions. And yes, when you start asking students to make decisions (e.g., how to study, what to study, or when to study), students will very likely make wrong or immature choices. That's okay! We learn to make decisions by making mistakes. Just because students make poor choices doesn't mean we should remove that responsibility altogether. Instead, use those poor choices (and outcomes) as an opportunity for self-evaluation and redirection.

As teachers, we tend to want class to run smoothly. We like things to be neat and tidy. Students are still learning how to live life, and the way they think and operate creates a hot mess in our classrooms. Instead of avoiding those messes, we've got to pull on our rubber boots and wade through the mess with them. Yes, it requires time and patience, but it's also how we can help them learn to make better decisions in the future.

What decisions do students *really* get to make in the class? Beyond completing assigned tasks, what are they responsible for?

Examples from the Classroom

Karen Mensing, a first and second grade teacher from Phoenix, Arizona, saw a compliance mentality creeping into her students when it came to technology. Instead of fixing all of their problems, she went to the source.

> *I created a "cyber squad" of a few responsible, tech-savvy students. These students helped other students when they were having a computer issue. The kids problem-solved together, which lessened interruptions to my teaching. The cyber squad students were extremely proud of this role and took it seriously.*

She was careful not to transfer the "putting out the fires" approach from her to her students. The students had to be good teachers, too.

> *I stressed that they needed to help the other students problem-solve and not just fix it for them. I had a class set of 1:1 Chromebooks, Nexus tablets, and iPads. Of course, nine times out of ten a reboot did the trick.*

Fifth-grade teacher Paul Solarz is the author of *Learn Like a PIRATE: Empower Your Students to Collaborate, Lead, and Succeed.* His emphasis on student-led classrooms (and reducing compliance mentality) helped him to be named to the top 50 of the 2015 Global Teacher Prize.

> *We naturally want to help kids learn, to be their providers and supporters, building background knowledge. We*

deprive them the opportunity to fail when we do that too much.

Wait a second. Is Paul suggesting that we provide, support, and help *less*?

Yes. That's *exactly* what he's suggesting.

If I do a little less here, they'll gain a lot more there in terms of life skills that they can transfer to other situations. You have to have the mindset that, yes, content is important, but I don't want to try to make straight A students out of everybody. I want them to also experience the struggle of learning and the problem-solving of figuring it out on their own.

His revelation came in a computer lab with more than twenty-five students. There were technical glitches galore, and Paul was exhausted running from student to student to fix their problems. Meanwhile, the students sat passively, waiting on him. He had become the bottleneck in his own classroom.

"At some point, I wondered why I'm putting out every fire when the kids can be putting out fires for us," he said. Just as with Karen Mensing, Paul's shift to student empowerment started in the computer lab. It continued from there to attendance and lunch count, checking students in, morning announcements, classroom activity set up, and student desk relocation.

He even empowered his students to stop the entire class at a moment's notice. He calls it "Gimme 5." If a student has information that everyone needs at that moment, that student is empowered to verbally declare a "Gimme 5" to get everyone's attention.

By empowering students to take risks and make decisions without permission, Paul has created a culture of action and responsibility.

His students aren't focused on pleasing their teacher to get a grade. There are standards and expectations of behavior, but the students help set those standards and expectations. As a result, Paul's students *own*—rather than rent—their education.

Measure Learning, Not Compliance

One day early in my teaching career, I (Alice) decided to analyze my gradebook and calculate how much of my students' grades were compliance-based. I made a spreadsheet. (Surprised? I like to say, "The answer is always a spreadsheet.") I figured out how many grades in the gradebook were not measures of learning. I came up with 30 percent.

Thirty percent! That is three letter grades!

Earlier, I wrote that it's common for students who most need the practice to refuse to do homework. I have also had students who knew the content very well but didn't complete their homework. Many times, they didn't feel like doing extra practice on something they thought they were proficient in. Other times, they just didn't want to do it. Their lack of compliance in completing their homework assignments meant they had to repeat algebra. Their grades weren't based on their ability. They were based on a lack of compliance. Other

> "My son is a voracious reader but forgets to fill out or have me sign his reading log so ends up with a C in reading while being a very advanced reader."
>
> —LAURIE ANASTASIO, PARENT AND THIRD GRADE TEACHER

students tried with all their hearts but still struggled with the content. Those students, though, did all their homework. Despite not having a grasp on the material, they graduated to geometry.

This was a colossal failure. The students who could do algebra were retained, but the ones who were good at playing "the game of school" moved on. Then a student asked me a question that perfectly described the problem: "Mrs. Keeler, what can I do to improve my grade that doesn't involve any work?"

Ah, the game of collecting points.

Grades should reflect what a student knows. No matter what grading system you use, remember it is *you* who assesses the student's final

DITCH THAT HOMEWORK RESOURCES

Want to shift your focus from compliance to learning? Consider moving to a standards-based gradebook. Traditional gradebooks focus on completing tasks and collecting points. There are lots of standards-based gradebooks available online. One option is to keep two gradebooks: one to measure learning and the other to track responsibility.

If your school requires a gradebook that is not standards-based, try this hack: Instead of listing assignments that you collect, list the learning objectives in the gradebook. This allows for students to demonstrate their learning in different ways, and you now have a place to put it in the gradebook. Rick Wormeli shares lots of great resources on standards-based grading on his website.

Standards-Based Grading Resources:
DitchThatHomework.com/wormeli

grade. If the grade in the gradebook does not match what the student knows, change it! There are many reasons the grades do not match what a student knows. Averaging grades is not an accurate measure of learning, and it records past failures. An F in the gradebook from the beginning of the term may not fairly represent what a student knows at the end of the term. If a student knows the material, scores that indicate otherwise result in an inaccurate measure of learning.

DITCH THE CHEATING

It is a well-known fact that students cheat. They copy each other's worksheets in the hall. You've seen it. We've seen it. We all know cheating happens. Once, I (Alice) assigned an online activity and a student told me, "You know, we just search the answer keys. They are all available online."

Trying to prevent cheating on homework is like playing "whack-a-mole." You may catch some, but you'll never catch them all. It's a game that you will *not* win. The real question is, *why do students cheat?* The answer: compliance. They know they have to turn in the assignment to receive a grade. They see the grade as the end goal. So what do some students see as the path of least resistance to get to the goal? Copy and cheat.

Let's get real for a second. How valuable is the work to the learning process when we know there is a likelihood of it being copied or cheated? When students can copy or cheat—and if they do—there is literally zero learning taking place. Every time a teacher asked me (Alice) to log something, I lied. My parents would lie with me, telling me to just sign their name on reading logs. Really, what does a parent signature mean other than the parents were around to sign it? If they didn't watch their child read, what are they actually signing?

"My bookworm daughter hated being told she HAD to read. Broke my heart."

—Nikki Vradenburg, fourth and fifth grade teacher

Compliance activities such as logs, worksheets, and other tasks perceived as busywork are not necessarily supported by parents. Parents don't want to spend their Wednesday nights figuring out the commutative property of multiplication. And when parents get frustrated that they don't remember how to do assignments at the middle school or high school level, they complain about how silly the work is, which doesn't help anyone. Worse yet, some parents just want to end the stress of homework, so they do the assignment for their kid. This happens—a lot.

Instead, let's do something that has proven positive effects: encourage independent reading. That's reading that reflects student choice, is done for information or pleasure, and is not assigned. In *School Library Media Research*, Bernice E. Cullinan of New York University points to research showing that independent reading promotes (Cullinan 2000):

- growth in vocabulary, reading comprehension and general information
- better readers, scoring higher on achievement tests
- better content knowledge in all subject areas

If there is a homework silver bullet, it seems to be independent reading. It's motivating to students because they have agency in what they choose. It's a favorite of parents because they don't need to help their children complete it. The problem, though, according to Cullinan, is that students don't often choose to do it, and as they get older, the amount they read tends to decrease. Programs to promote independent reading show promise, like read-alouds, book borrowing and discussion groups.

"What I have always seen as a teacher is a lot of absolutely perfect homework returned to me: homework that a first grader certainly couldn't have done and is nothing like the work he presents in class. What is the point of giving homework if a parent is going to complete it? My best example: Students had to finish a story at home via Google Docs. I had the kids open up the Doc in class the next day and one boy (a first grade student) seemed shocked at the content on his. He said, "My mom must have done this after I went to bed." I checked the revision history and the work had been completed very late at night."

—KAREN MENSING, FIRST AND SECOND GRADE TEACHER

DITCH THAT HOMEWORK RESOURCES

Shaelynn Farnsworth offers Six Alternatives to Reading Logs

1. **BookSnaps**

   Have students on social media share what they've read. Using Snapchat, Instagram, or even a class feed in Seesaw or Google Classroom, students can snap pictures and annotate as they read. This can be scaffolded with daily prompts or independent posts where students share what they want in each post. Go global by sharing on Twitter using the hashtag #BookSnaps.

2. **Book Blogs**

   Book Blogs provide students the experience of sharing what they read with a global audience. Replacing the traditional reading journal with a digital one, Book Blogs are a contemporary alternative and help promote both reading and writing.

3. **Vlogs**

   Along with Book Blogs, students can create vlogs to share what they've read. Through short videos, students can illustrate their progress and demonstrate their understanding.

4. **PCI (Passage, Connection, Illustration)**

   As adults, when we read something we enjoy, we talk about it. Make reading social again with book discussions. Help students prepare by using the PCI strategy.

   Passage: Choose a powerful passage from your book that caught your attention, moved you, or made you wonder.

Connection: How did you personally connect to the text? What did it remind you of? Are there any other books you have read that are similar to this one? Tell stories.

Illustration: Draw or create a picture or infographic that represents this book.

5. **Give Me 5**

   Give Me 5 is a simple strategy where students choose five quotes from the book that best illustrate the author's message, insight into a character, or conceptual understanding. These quotes almost always lead to excellent reflection and discussion in the classroom.

6. **Concept Mapping**

   Concept mapping is an opportunity for students to make their thinking visible. It allows readers to connect characters and events to larger concepts by synthesizing, evaluating, and organizing their thoughts. Concept mapping moves students past surface-level comprehension to digging deeply into text.

While none of the above alternatives track minutes spent reading, all of them align to the reason many educators use reading logs in the first place. Focus on the why instead of the how of instruction. Lifelong readers are not made by minute tracking; lifelong readers are cultivated through experiences with the stories they read!

Find Shaelynn Farnsworth on Twitter at @shfarnsworth or at shaelynnfarnsworth.com.

How can we be sure students are doing their own work? Watch them do it. If you value it, make time for it in class. If it results in minimal learning, ditch it.

TEACH FOR MASTERY

If students do an assignment, get a grade, and maybe receive a feedback comment, the grade ends the learning process. We know all too well that students rarely read the comments we put in the margins of their papers. Why? Because they are mentally *done* with the project. Even if they do read the comments, they aren't likely to internalize or learn from them. The truth is, they're thinking, *why are you still talking if we're done with this? Go on to the next thing.*

If a student earns a low score and we just move on, the message the student internalizes is that the content wasn't really all that important. Beyond grades and time spent on a unit, hopefully what matters most is how much the students learn. Let's not let our classes be about "going on to the next thing." Let's ensure that our students know we value learning. Above grades, above compliance, mastery is what matters.

Students used to ask me, "Mrs. Keeler, can't I just get a D?"

"Nope," I would answer. "Have to keep working on this until you get it."

In moving to mastery learning, students are expected to keep working on something until they have met minimum proficiencies. Be careful, though. Reteaching the same thing in the same way is ineffective. When students need to revisit a topic, try either approaching it in a different way or finding a different way for students to demonstrate their knowledge. If you need a change of pace, have students explain or teach to the rest of the class. Just hearing it in someone else's words is often enough to unlock understanding for some students.

"I stopped assigning homework when I moved to a mastery learning environment. The big change for me was not assigning work for class and work for home. Instead, I focused only on learning and gave students lots of options on how/when they wanted to learn and how they wanted to demonstrate mastery. In the end, there was no more classwork or homework, there was just learning and that could happen wherever the student was most comfortable. Many students did a lot of that at home anyway because they wanted to, while some students never did any work at home because they were able to show mastery while only working during class."

—MICHAEL NASH, TEACHER

Assessment of mastery does not have to be a test—especially if it's the *same* assessment that showed the students' weakness. Often, students know what they're trying to learn. They just have a hard time showing it. When we let students show mastery in the way that fits them best—in a one-on-one meeting or through their creative talents— they're empowered instead of belittled.

TEACH FOR MASTERY

(1) SET MINIMUM PROFICIENCY 🏃

Not learning something is not an option. At a minimum what should a student be able to do to be able to move on?

(2) CHOOSE WHAT TO ASSESS ⚃

What assignments measure learning and mastery of a concept? Not everything has to be graded or assessed.

(3) EMBRACE FAILURE 🗎

If it's not an assessment for mastery, don't grade it. It's formative. Allow students to try different ideas without the fear of damaging their grade.

(4) RETEACH DIFFERENTLY ∞

Don't do the same thing and expect different results. When students are not meeting proficiency, consider new approaches.

(5) SIT WITH A KID 🪑

Talking AT the class is efficient but the most effective way to reach a kid is to sit with them.

(6) DEVELOP GRIT 🧗

Help students develop grit that they can and will learn something even if it takes time.

Icons: Numero Uno, Desbenoit, Penny Wongpaibool, Juraj Sedlák, Hea Poh Lin, Focus Lab, IYIKON via TheNounProject.com

DITCH THAT HOMEWORK

Don't Practice Wrong

Students do a lot of practice for the sake of practice. It's like throwing spaghetti at a wall to see if it's done; we hope it's going to stick. If students know how to do the work, they don't need significant amounts of extra practice. If they don't know how to do the work, practicing wrong can cause damage. How much should a student do wrong before receiving intervention? It is soul sucking to do a page of work only to find out later it was wrong. Imagine the conversation that ensues:

Teacher: "*Can you redo that?*"

Student: "*Ugh … no.*"

The problem with paper-based homework is that it doesn't offer the timely feedback that is vital to students' learning and subsequent success. Think of what happens when we give students homework to take home with no support—and no context for reflecting on learning. With a focus just on repetition and memorization, students end up practicing things the wrong way. It's like driving south on a north-bound trip—counterintuitive to their learning as a whole.

Why ditch compliance? Well, making teachers' lives easier is not a reason to do it. It's easier to photocopy worksheets, hand them out, and demand their completion the next day than it is to break the compliance mold.

What kind of learners does compliance create? Yep, compliant ones. And the marketplace isn't looking for compliance. It craves people with creative minds who can solve problems, communicate, and think for themselves. When we, as teachers, turn away from rhetoric and compliance and focus on action and independent thinking, we help make lifelong learning a reality.

"With my special ed students, I have found that about half of them never did any homework (even if they totally understood the concept), so it would drastically bring their grade down. The students who did not understand would complete the homework problems all wrong, which was basically reinforcing solving the problem incorrectly, making it harder to undo the damage. I would rather have them practicing more in class where I can head off errors or provide more rigorous problems to those who are successful."

—Caryn Trautz, teacher

Ditch That Homework Resources

When considering digital practice, look for resources that provide students feedback question by question. The effectiveness of the self-grading tool is reduced when the feedback is given at the end of the practice.

- IXL math (ixl.com/math)
- Quia (quia.com)
- Kahoot! (getkahoot.com)
- Formative (goformative.com)
- Quizziz (quizizz.com)
- Revision assistant by Turnitin (turnitin.com/en_us/what-we-offer/revision-assistant)

CHAPTER 8
Ditch That Red Pen

Provide Timely, Meaningful Feedback that Students Can Really Use

AS A HIGH SCHOOL SPANISH TEACHER, I (MATT) KNEW THAT HAVING MY STUDENTS WRITE WAS IMPORTANT TO THEIR DEVELOPMENT IN THE LANGUAGE. I knew, however, that writing for an "audience of one" wasn't very motivating for my students. Nor was the promise of a grade. But if my students knew that dozens of people would be reading their work, I felt certain they would be more motivated to do their best.

So we started blogging. Students created their own blogs where they could post content. Using their Chromebooks, they would write about a topic in class where they could ask questions to one another or me.

At first, I figured that if they wrote digitally, I should provide feedback digitally. Students wrote their blog posts and then submitted them to me. I would later open up their work and write comments with any feedback I had to share—positive and constructive.

After grading their work in this way for several assignments, something became painfully clear to me. No one was reading my comments. No one. I might as well have been shouting them into the wind. I put in all of this time outside of class to provide meaningful feedback, and it was falling on deaf ears.

This is a fatal flaw of traditional homework. The feedback loop is way too long. Students complete an assignment and turn it in. Then, we return it with comments and corrections about the next day. (That's assuming that we were able to turn them around in twenty-four hours!) But as Alice pointed out in the previous chapter, most of the time, students are mentally done with an assignment as soon as they turn it in.

OFFER MEANINGFUL FEEDBACK

Think about the delay in receiving feedback. Imagine if students received an assignment, worked on the assignment the night it was assigned, and turned it in the next day. From the moment they cognitively wrestled with that work to the moment they got feedback on it, as many as forty-eight hours had passed. When they get that delayed feedback, what they really want to tell you is, "Come on … I've slept twice since then!"

It takes work for anyone—child or adult—to go back to their thought processes from two days before. If the choice is between throwing an assignment away and doing the kind of hard thinking necessary to apply slow feedback from a teacher, is there any wonder so many homework assignments end up in the recycle bin?

THE HOMEWORK CYCLE

The feedback loop for traditional homework assignment

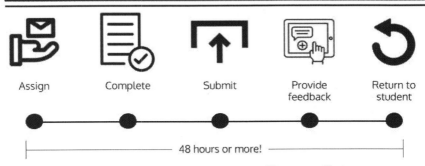

| Assign | Complete | Submit | Provide feedback | Return to student |

48 hours or more!

Icons by MRFA, Oliviu Stoian, bezier master, Hector, Creative Stall, Kaylen Quek via TheNounProject.com

DITCH THAT HOMEWORK

I found a simple alternative that was immensely more effective than those digital blog comments. It was a very low-tech alternative, too, that you may be familiar with. I have a very fancy term for it. It's called "walking around the room."

I walked up and down the rows in my classroom, looking at student screens as they worked. I stopped at each student's desk and sandwiched suggestions within compliments. Our discussions sounded something like this:

> *Wow, look at that. You used that word in your blog post and we haven't covered that in months. Good memory! Now remember, in this sentence you'll want to use the word* por *instead of* para *because it's talking about a period of time. But all in all, I really like the direction you're taking in your writing. Keep up the great work!*

PROVIDE USEFUL FEEDBACK

(1) MAKE IT TIMELY

Slow feedback doesn't get internalized much. It's why graded work ends up in the trash can. Do it immediately when possible.

(2) LEVERAGE AUTOMATION

Many digital tools let you give students comments and explanations while they work.

(3) DON'T DO TOO MUCH

A paper soaking in red ink is soul-sucking. Plus, it's too much to adjust all at once. Pick and choose your feedback.

(4) MAKE IT A GAME

Amazing feedback can come through play. Have fun with practice, and make feedback a natural part of the game.

(5) USE A PERSONAL TOUCH

Sitting down shoulder to shoulder with a student to explain builds relationships and individualizes learning.

(6) GO DEEP

Lots of shallow comments don't have the same impact as thorough comments on one answer.

AVOID OVERWHELM AND SHUT-DOWN

As I walked around the room and offered comments, I boiled my suggestions down to one key point I wanted that student to remember. Were there other mistakes I wanted to correct? Oh boy, you'd better believe there were! So why didn't I correct them? Why did I limit my feedback to one key point?

Here's what I've found with feedback on assignments. Often, we bombard students with too much of it. Students will see all of that red ink (or metaphorical "red ink" on a screen) and will mentally and emotionally shut down. They'll be overwhelmed with all of those changes. Plus, if they're like me, they'll turn inward with those corrections and start to question their abilities and, in turn, their self-worth. When students feel like failures, they lose their motivation to improve. In this situation, I found that one or two corrections or suggestions per conversation was the right number to help students grow and to encourage them at the same time.

Whether they'll admit it or not, many students crave feedback. They want to know how their work stacks up. They want to see if they've progressed. No, let's correct that. They want to see *that* they *have* progressed. They want to know where they stand. They're *hoping* they have made strides forward in their learning, and they want your affirmation and guidance.

When we assign students traditional homework, they're at a disadvantage from a feedback standpoint. Among other reasons, they often aren't getting timely feedback—at the point when they're cognitively wrestling with their work. Plus, they aren't getting the comments, encouragement, and guidance they crave when feedback is reduced to a check mark or an X over their incorrect answers.

If students get solid, personalized, and timely feedback, they know their strengths and areas to improve. They know where they stand, and they know how to get to the next level.

So how can we improve on the "mark up homework assignments" model of feedback? And how can providing quality feedback help us reduce our dependence on homework to the point we may be able to ditch it? Here are some ideas.

Automate Grading

I (Alice) have a rule. If the computer can grade it, it should.

Sending students home to do non-digital work can be frustrating for the student and can create paperwork for the teacher. This is a *lose-lose* scenario. This assumes that the student knows the material well enough to do the work independently—an assumption that can set students back. They may do work incorrectly and practice doing it wrong. And as they say, practice makes permanent. Sure, we can show students how to do the work correctly and ask them to redo the assignment, but that's frustrating and demoralizing. And redoing homework is rarely welcomed by a student.

If students are doing the work digitally, they are able to receive immediate feedback from you, the computer, or from their peers. Students know immediately if they are on the right track. If they get a problem incorrect, they can try to figure out why and tackle a second problem. Similarly, doing this independent practice in class allows students to get help when they need it, which reduces frustration and increases motivation.

Go Deep Instead of Broad

We've said it before: Rigor is not defined by quantity. Less can be more. Having students analyze a few concepts or go deep with feedback conversations on a handful of questions can yield more learning than answering lots of questions with lower critical thinking. Allow students to tackle a complex problem and to contrast with non-examples ("The rule doesn't fit here because …") and unusual cases ("We do something different here because …").

Math teacher Diana Herrington uses this philosophy of deep thinking. Instead of assigning a huge set of problems from the text, she allows students to choose three problems for the week—the *whole* week. The students do these three problems in Google Slides. They explain their thinking step by step and go deeper with each problem to focus on and model understanding.

Diana doesn't assess learning based on getting the right answer. Instead, she focuses on the feedback conversation. At first, students attempt the easy questions. She provides feedback comments in their Google Slides and asks questions to further their thinking. Then, they revise and refine their thinking. This back-and-forth conversation increases student confidence and promotes understanding more so than if they had done a page of problems in isolation. They become better risk takers. Before long, Diana's students shift to choosing the hardest problems in the text.

You can only give high-quality feedback on so much work before getting burned out. If you're initiating this process for the first time in your classroom, pick one assignment at a time that you will give feedback on over a particular period of time. The feedback loop is to allow the students to think, receive feedback, and respond to or reflect on the feedback. It may take several iterations to ensure that students have a firm understanding of the material.

Make Learning Last

In Chapter 5, we talked about how we can make learning stick if students practice retrieval and spaced repetition. Part of the reason this cycle of learning and recall is so effective is that they're getting timely feedback in regular intervals. Plenty of formative assessment tools on the web, plus engaging non-tech practice exercises in the classroom, can provide that all-important timely feedback.

Jon Corippo, director of academic innovation for CUE, believes *repping* in class is a far better strategy than assigning homework. "Why the heck are kids just quietly writing down spelling words? Why are we doing word searches for homework? What we should be doing is repping in class. I think *that* is magical."

What Jon is suggesting is spaced repetition—and making it fun! Here's how:

First, create a series of questions and set them up in a fun game-style format, like a Quizizz game or Socrative's Space Race, and let the students play. But here is the wrinkle: Do it on Monday, before any direct instruction or lecture. After students complete all of the questions, the teacher immediately puts student results on a projector screen. As Jon points out, "Quizizz grades things automatically. #NoneMinutes." Discuss the questions that the students scored lowest on so they can improve. An immediate mini-lesson ensues on material where students struggle. Feedback is almost instant. Bonus: If the class even gets half correct, the cognitive load for the new content is limited. *Bam!* You only need to "teach" half as much content.

Then, have the kids play the game again. Yes, the exact same game. With the same questions. Students are able to apply the lesson they just learned seconds prior. They check their results afterward and see that they've improved. They've applied their learning, reflected on their performance, adjusted their approach, and applied their changes immediately. Watch for improvement on the *class* average; don't worry about individuals. "If I can fix what the class is bad at, I'm fixing what the individuals are bad at," Jon says.

Imagine the power of doing those game-based, quick assessment activities twice a day Monday through Wednesday. Then, give the whole class a test on Thursday. If the class average is above 90 percent, give the whole class an A, and then you've earned your Friday back. (If the "give everyone A's if the class is above 90 percent" isn't your thing, come up with your own version of scoring.)

Every teacher craves time. This flow eliminates at *least* one full class period a week of lecture time for new (albeit low-level) concepts. It eliminates the need to give students very low-level homework. Ask yourself, "What can I do with 20 percent more instructional time per *week* for the rest of my career?"

Now, Jon explains, we don't have to send those kids home with homework because of those efficient, effective repetitions with quick, meaningful feedback. In contrast, think about a worksheet full of math problems, Spanish verb conjugations, or comprehension questions from a reading.

How many times do students answer those questions? *Once.*

How much feedback do they get while they're still locked into that assignment? *None.* That worksheet can't talk back to them.

How much reflection do they do when they've finished? *None.*

How invested are they in that worksheet and, in turn, learning from it? *Not very much.*

Where is the "mastery"? *Not in the worksheet.* A one-time test is not a strong indicator that kids *"own"* their learning. (Hat tip to educational technology leader Alan November for that idea.)

Ditch That Homework Resources

Folder with picture images   Click Chrome extension   Google Slides automatically created from photos.

Ditch That Homework has created a Chrome extension to take a folder of images in Google Drive and magically turn them into a Google Slides presentation. If your images or screenshots are not already in Google Drive, create a folder in Drive and add images to it. If you have images in Google Drive, make sure they are in a folder. You may want to create a subfolder just for the images you wish to add to the Google Slides presentation.

DriveSlides Chrome Extension:
DitchThatHomework.com/driveslides

There's value to working, practicing, doing repetitions in class. A highly skilled teacher is there to provide personalized, pointed, timely feedback. We know how the repetitions are getting done and students are getting the cues and reminders they need.

We often think that *more* practice is better, that practice in class *plus* practice at home equals better learning. That's dangerous thinking. Half-hearted attempts in class plus half-hearted attempts at home do not equal wholehearted learning. Let's consider doing that practice to the best of our ability *once* instead of having to redo it over and over and over again.

Sit with a Student

Technology allows me (Alice) to better spread feedback around to students all over the classroom. For example, I can create a Google Slides presentation and share it with all of my students via Google Classroom. All of my students then open that presentation and set up their own slide on it. That way, they can see what everyone is doing, which creates the perfect environment for peer feedback. Students add a blank slide into the same Google Slides presentation and, just as I would with individual whiteboards, have students write something or work out a math problem.

Once students have started the assignment, I scan the room and check in verbally with the students, getting them on task. Some typical comments: "Do you need some help getting started?" "Are you on your slide working?" "Is the Chromebook charged??"

Then, I pick up my chair, carry it across the room and sit down next to a kid. We'll check over what they need to do to get started, and I'll give that student some feedback.

If students are in groups, when giving feedback to one student the entire group benefits. Then, I pick up my chair, carry it to another part of the classroom, and sit down next to another student. Same routine.

After I've done this twice, I'll head back to my own computer. Wanting to be quick and get back to sitting with students, I do not sit down at my computer. I'll find a slide on that Google Slides presentation and add a comment. (It's kind of like a little sticky note that appears next to their slide where I can type.) I'll write some quick feedback to the student in the comment. A lot of text isn't necessary; typing "You need a simile" is better than six sentences about the importance of similes and how they can best be used in writing. In fact, just write, "Simile needed." Shorter is better!

I repeat this process: survey room, sit next to a student, sit next to a student, insert feedback comment, insert feedback comment. There's lots of quick feedback while students are working on it. In this case, *just in time* feedback is more effective than *just in case* feedback.

When I'm writing comments on students' work in the slide presentation, I don't write comments on every single slide. Often, there just aren't enough minutes in class for that. But here's the beauty of this assignment: Everybody sees all the comments. We're all on the same slide presentation, so everyone can see one another's slides.

This is the culture of our classroom. Not only do my students expect feedback from me, they expect it from their peers as well. And peer feedback is so powerful. We're a community of learners, and we help one another get better. Students see others' work and write comments to critique, guide, and help. In this kind of classroom culture, students are going to be getting feedback. It just might not be from the teacher every time.

What happens when I'm not providing *all* of the feedback? It gives me time to focus on critical thinking and to encourage students. It also gives me time to build relationships with my students. In the activity I've described, the best part isn't the instruction I'm delivering. It's the relationships that I'm developing with my students.

The most important thing I can do as a teacher is sit next to a kid. When I'm providing that quick, instant feedback and letting students do the work themselves, it frees me up to sit with them and build positive relationships. That's the best and highest use of my time.

Meaningful feedback is the key to unlocking more time in class. When students get feedback in a timely manner, they can actually use it. They can apply it to what they're doing in that moment. When they get face-to-face feedback, it's personal. Plus, when they can see that their teacher really cares for them, it builds relationships. All of that leads to a more effective, more efficient classroom. And when you have that extra efficiency and learning improves, the reliance on homework goes down to the point that you can ditch it all together.

CONCLUSION

WE'VE COVERED A LOT. In eight chapters, we have encouraged you to …

"Ditch That Textbook," replacing tired, "textbook" activities like worksheets and research papers with something newer, fresher, and more relevant.

"Ditch That Lecture," evaluating your teaching style to include instructional practices that will stimulate, engage, and prepare students effectively.

"Ditch That Referral," building relationships with parents, with students, and among students to increase harmony and sense of value.

"Ditch That Resistance," recruiting parents to become strong allies at home, working together in pursuit of helping their children thrive.

"Ditch Those Habits," tapping into the power of the brain and brain-friendly learning.

"Ditch That Remediation," instilling strong skills and habits to reinforce what students have learned to prepare them for the future.

"Ditch That Compliance," helping students learn to be responsible and accountable for their own learning.

"Ditch That Red Pen," providing students with the right kind of instant feedback that they can use to improve and put it to use right away.

Ultimately, it's up to you to decide where you'll stand with homework—whether you're working to reduce your reliance on it or are ready to ditch it completely. Either way, it's time to take some action.

Here are some steps you can take now.

Take it a step at a time. Alice and I (Matt) work with teachers all the time, encouraging them to try new things in their classrooms that will move the learning needle, and our advice is to move forward, but don't rush it. If you move too fast, you'll overwhelm your students *and* yourself. I've seen it happen in my own classroom, and it's a recipe for burnout. Proceed at a moderate pace. Don't move so slowly that you're complacent and there's no progress toward your goals, but don't be like the overzealous rabbit in *The Tortoise and the Hare*, either.

Keep everyone in the loop. No one likes to be caught off guard. If you're ready to make significant changes with homework (or anything, for that matter), the worst time to announce it is Day 1 with the first assignment. Let the students know what's coming. Inform their parents. And for heaven's sake, let your school leadership know. Talk to them. No, talk *with* them. Help them understand the value in what you envision. Share small successes, as those will provide the confidence your stakeholders will need to take the next step.

Be open minded. Not every change that's best for your students is going to be *your thing*. That doesn't mean that it isn't best. Listen to people who have different ideas from you. Evaluate their ideas and decide if they're best for your students.

In our discussions with educators about ditching homework, one from Jon Corippo has stuck with me. Jon helped create an innovative high school in California that had a policy of "no dumb homework." A visitor to the school asked a student about homework once. The student thought about it for a second and said, "We don't have any homework. We do a lot of projects, though." The secret behind that, Jon said, was that the students were passionate enough about their projects that they *wanted* to work on them at home.

Here's the comment from Jon that stuck with me: "*I think we're going to have to go through a middle phase before we go to no homework.*"

If we're deeply entrenched in a homework-rich school culture, it won't be easy to make a transition. It will probably be next to impossible to do it immediately. Identify the situation. Take logical steps to get to where you want to be. In the end, no matter how you ditch your homework, there's one question that should be at the heart of it all:

What's best for the kids?

Programs aren't what make school successful. People are. When we have big goals, it's easy to get focused on our plans and to try not to deviate from them. When we do that, we dehumanize the process. The whole reason we got into education is to help kids become fantastic adults. When we lose sight of them, it's like losing the *true north* on a compass. We start to lose our way.

As you embark on your homework ditching process, remember that change is a lot like pushing a huge boulder. We lean on that boulder, push that boulder, and become exhausted trying to move that boulder. It may seem like it's not going anywhere. But often, it's the moment that we most want to give up that is the most crucial; that's the moment when we're getting close to a breakthrough. Then, the boulder budges. We keep pushing, and a budge becomes a roll. The rolling picks up speed, and suddenly, the boulder is rolling down the hill with unstoppable force.

Don't give up just because the boulder doesn't seem to budge.

In the end, it's up to us to craft the educational experiences that prepare students for the future.

Be brave. Be creative and innovative. And take action, starting *now*.

Go ahead. You know you want to.

Ditch That Homework!

ACKNOWLEDGMENTS

Thank you to the following people for their help and support in making this book happen:

Educators Karen Mensing, Shaelynn Farnsworth, Karly Moura, Jim Bentley, the #DitchBook Twitter chat crew, Jon Corippo, and countless others. (You know who you are.)

Our spouses, Melanie Miller and Barton Keeler, who are our sounding boards, our support systems and our rocks in times of trouble.

To the late Diana Herrington who has inspired my (Alice) innovation and greatly influenced my teaching practices.

Our publishers, Dave and Shelley Burgess, whose unconditional support and belief in us empowered us to take this passion and create something to help teachers.

OUR PLN! Thanks to all of you who contributed through Twitter and Facebook—and those who answered our surveys. Your help made this book a truly collaborative process!

REFERENCES

Afflerback, Peter, David Pearson, and Scott G. Paris. "Clarifying Differences between Reading Skills and Reading Strategies." The Reading Teacher 61, no. 5 (2008): 364-373. doi:10.1598/RT.61.5.1

Barr, Robert and John Tagg. 1995. "From Teaching to Learning—A New Paradigm for Undergraduate Education." *Change: The Magazine of Higher Learning.* 27(6): 12-25. DOI:10.1598

Battaglia, Floriana and Lucio Bontempelli. (2014). "Does Homework Increase Students' Autonomy?" *International Conference: New Perspectives in Science Education Abstract:* 286. conference.pixel-online.net/NPSE/acceptedabstracts_scheda.php?id_abs=243.

Brown, Peter C., Henry L. Roediger, and Mark A. McDaniel. 2014. *Make it Stick.* Harvard University Press.

Corno, Lyn. 1996. "Homework Is a Complicated Thing." *Educational Researcher,* 25(8): 27-30.

Cooper, Harris. 1989. "Synthesis of Research on Homework." *Educational Leadership,* 47(3): 85-91.

Cullinan, Bernice E. "Independent Reading and School Achievement." *School Library Media Research* 3, no. 3 (2000).

DeLong, Suzanne. 2009. "Teaching Methods to Encourage Independent Learning and Thinking." *Submitted as partial fulfillment of Master Teacher Program, Center for Teaching Excellence, United States Military Academy, West Point, NY.* Retrieved from westpoint.edu/cfe/Literature/DeLongS_09.pdf

Dweck, Carol S., Gregory Walton, and Geoffrey Cohen. 2011. "Academic tenacity: Mindsets and skills that promote long-term learning." *Gates Foundation.* Bill & Melinda Gates Foundation: Seattle, WA.

Elliott, Elaine S., and Carol Dweck. 1988. "Goals: An Approach to Motivation and Achievement." *Journal of Personality and Social Psychology*, 54(1): 5.

Field, Tiffany, Diego Miguel, and Christopher E. Sanders. 2001. "Exercise is Positively Related to Adolescents' Relationships and Academics." *Adolescence,* 36(141): 105.

Gillen–O'Neel, C., V.W. Huynh, and A.J. Fuligni. 2013. "To Study or to Sleep? The Academic Costs of Extra Studying at the Expense of Sleep." *Child Development*, 84(1): 133-142.

Husmann, Polly R., J. Bradley Barger, and Audra Schutte. 2016. "Study Skills in Anatomy and Physiology: Is There a Difference?" *Anatomical Sciences Education*, 9(1):18-27.

Jensen, Eric, ed. 2008. *Super Teaching: Over 1000 Practical Strategies.* Corwin Press, 2008.

Karpicke, Jeffrey D., and Janell R. Blunt. 2011. "Retrieval Practice Produces More Learning Than Elaborative Studying with Concept Mapping." *Science* 331.6018: 772-775.

Kohl III, Harold W. and Heather D. Cook, eds. 2013. *Educating the Student Body: Taking Physical Activity and Physical Education to School*. National Academies Press.

Kohn, Alfie. 2007. *The Homework Myth: Why Our Kids Get Too Much of a Bad Thing*. De Capo Press: Philadelphia.

Lindsay, D. Stephen, et al. 2014. *Remembering: Attributions, Processes, and Control in Human Memory*. Psychology Press: New York, London.

Mehring, Jeff and Regan Thomson. 2016. "Brain-Friendly Learning Tips for Long-Term Retention and Recall." *Language Teacher*, 40: 9.

Miller, Claire Cain. "Stressed, Tired, Rushed: A Portrait of the Modern Family." *New York Times* (New York, NY), Nov. 4, 2015.

Nicol, David J. and Debra Macfarlane-Dick. 2006. "Formative Assessment and Self-regulated Learning: A Model and Seven Principles of Good Feedback Practice." *Studies in Higher Education*, 31(2): 199-218.

Pappas, Peter. "Teachers, Have the Courage to be Less Helpful." Copy/Paste, July 19, 2011. peterpappas.com/2011/07/teachers-have-courage-to-be-less-helpful.html.

Peterson, Sarah E. 1991. "The Cognitive Functions of Underlining as a Study Technique." *Literacy Research and Instruction*, 31(2): 49-56.

Richardson, Michelle, Charles Abraham, and Rod Bond. 2012. "Psychological Correlates of University Students' Academic Performance: A Systematic Review and Meta-analysis." *Psychological Bulletin*, 138(2): 353-387. doi: 10.1037/a0026838.

Sattelmair, Jacob, and John J. Ratey. 2009. "Physically Active Play and Cognition: An Academic Matter?" *American Journal of Play* 1(3): 365-374.

Sefton-Green, Julian. 2004. "Literature Review in Informal Learning with Technology Outside School." nfer.ac.uk/publications/FUTL72/FUTL72.pdf.

Sibley, Benjamin A. and Jennifer L. Etnier. 2003. "The Relationship between Physical Activity and Cognition in Children: a Meta-analysis." *Pediatric Exercise Science,* 15(3): 243-256.

Sisti, Helene M., Arnold L. Glass, and Tracey J. Shors. 2007. "Neurogenesis and the Spacing Effect: Learning over Time Enhances Memory and the Survival of New Neurons." *Learning & Memory,* 14(5): 368-375.

Tucker, Catlin. 2016. "Who Is Doing the Work in Your Classroom?" Catlin Tucker Blog, November 8. catlintucker.com/2016/11/who-is-doing-the-work/.

Wallace, K. "Kids Have Three Times Too Much Homework, Study Finds." *CNN.com*, August 12, 2015. cnn.com/2015/08/12/health/homework-elementary-school-study/.

Wernersbach, Brenna, Susan Crowley, Scott C. Bates, and Carol Rosenthal. 2014. "Study Skills Course Impact on Academic Self-efficacy." *Journal of Developmental Education, 37*(2), 14-16.

MORE FROM
DAVE BURGESS
Consulting, inc.

Teach Like a PIRATE

Increase Student Engagement, Boost Your Creativity, and Transform Your Life as an Educator
By Dave Burgess (@BurgessDave)

Teach Like a PIRATE is the New York Times' best-selling book that has sparked a worldwide educational revolution. It is part inspirational manifesto that ignites passion for the profession and part practical road map, filled with dynamic strategies to dramatically increase student engagement. Translated into multiple languages, its message resonates with educators who want to design outrageously creative lessons and transform school into a life-changing experience for students.

Learn Like a PIRATE

Empower Your Students to Collaborate, Lead, and Succeed

By Paul Solarz (@PaulSolarz)

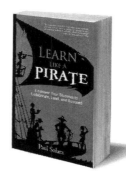

Today's job market demands that students be prepared to take responsibility for their lives and careers. We do them a disservice if we teach them how to earn passing grades without equipping them to take charge of their education. In *Learn Like a PIRATE*, Paul Solarz explains how to design classroom experiences that encourage students to take risks and explore their passions in a stimulating, motivating, and supportive environment where improvement, rather than grades, is the focus. Discover how student-led classrooms help students thrive and develop into self-directed, confident citizens who are capable of making smart, responsible decisions, all on their own.

P is for PIRATE

Inspirational ABC's for Educators

By Dave and Shelley Burgess (@Burgess_Shelley)

Teaching is an adventure that stretches the imagination and calls for creativity every day! In *P is for PIRATE*, husband and wife team Dave and Shelley Burgess encourage and inspire educators to make their classrooms fun and exciting places to learn. Tapping into years of personal experience and drawing on the insights of more than seventy educators, the authors offer a wealth of ideas for making learning and teaching more fulfilling than ever before.

Play Like a Pirate

Engage Students with Toys, Games, and Comics. Make Your Classroom Fun Again!

By Quinn Rollins (@jedikermit)

Yes! School can be simultaneously fun and educational. In *Play Like a Pirate*, Quinn Rollins offers practical, engaging strategies and resources that make it easy to integrate fun into your curriculum. Regardless of the grade level you teach, you'll find inspiration and ideas that will help you engage your students in unforgettable ways.

eXPlore Like a Pirate

Gamification and Game-Inspired Course Design to Engage, Enrich, and Elevate Your Learners

By Michael Matera (@MrMatera)

Are you ready to transform your classroom into an experiential world that flourishes on collaboration and creativity? Then set sail with classroom game designer and educator Michael Matera as he reveals the possibilities and power of game-based learning. In *eXPlore Like a Pirate*, Matera serves as your experienced guide to help you apply the most motivational techniques of gameplay to your classroom. You'll learn gamification strategies that will work with and enhance (rather than replace) your current curriculum and discover how these engaging methods can be applied to any grade level or subject.

The Innovator's Mindset

Empower Learning, Unleash Talent,
and Lead a Culture of Creativity

By George Couros (@gcouros)

The traditional system of education requires students to hold their questions and compliantly stick to the scheduled curriculum. But our job as educators is to provide new and better opportunities for our students. It's time to recognize that compliance doesn't foster innovation, encourage critical thinking, or inspire creativity—and those are the skills our students need to succeed. In *The Innovator's Mindset*, George Couros encourages teachers and administrators to empower their learners to wonder, to explore—and to become forward-thinking leaders.

Master the Media

How Teaching Media Literacy Can
Save Our Plugged-in World

By Julie Smith (@julnilsmith)

Written to help teachers and parents educate the next generation, *Master the Media* explains the history, purpose, and messages behind the media. The point isn't to get kids to unplug; it's to help them make informed choices, understand the difference between truth and lies, and discern perception from reality. Critical thinking leads to smarter decisions—and it's why media literacy can save the world.

The Zen Teacher

Creating FOCUS, SIMPLICITY, and
TRANQUILITY in the Classroom

By Dan Tricarico (@TheZenTeacher)

Teachers have incredible power to influence—even improve—the future. In *The Zen Teacher*, educator, blogger, and speaker Dan Tricarico provides practical, easy-to-use techniques to help teachers be their best—unrushed and fully focused—so they can maximize their performance and improve their quality of life. In this introductory guide, Dan Tricarico explains what it means to develop a Zen practice—something that has nothing to do with religion and everything to do with your ability to thrive in the classroom.

Lead Like a PIRATE

Make School Amazing for Your Students and Staff

By Shelley Burgess and Beth Houf
(@Burgess_Shelley, @BethHouf)

In *Lead Like a PIRATE*, education leaders Shelley Burgess and Beth Houf map out the character traits necessary to captain a school or district. You'll learn where to find the treasure that's already in your classrooms and schools—and how to bring out the very best in your educators. This book will equip and encourage you to be relentless in your quest to make school amazing for your students, staff, parents, and communities.

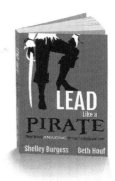

50 Things You Can Do with Google Classroom

By Alice Keeler and Libbi Miller
(@AliceKeeler, @MillerLibbi)

It can be challenging to add new technology to the classroom, but it's a must if students are going to be well-equipped for the future. Alice Keeler and Libbi Miller shorten the learning curve by providing a thorough over-view of the Google Classroom App. Part of Google Apps for Education (GAfE), Google Classroom was specifically designed to help teachers save time by streamlining the process of going digital. Complete with screenshots, *50 Things You Can Do with Google Classroom* provides ideas and step-by-step instructions to help teachers implement this powerful tool.

50 Things to Go Further with Google Classroom

A Student-Centered Approach

By Alice Keeler and Libbi Miller
(@AliceKeeler, @MillerLibbi)

Today's technology empowers educators to move away from the traditional classroom where teachers lead and students work independently—each doing the same thing. In *50 Things to Go Further with Google Classroom: A Student-Centered Approach*, authors and educators Alice Keeler and Libbi Miller offer inspiration and resources to help you create a digitally rich, engaging, student-centered environment. They show you how to tap into the power of individualized learning that is possible with Google Classroom.

Pure Genius

Building a Culture of Innovation and
Taking 20% Time to the Next Level

By Don Wettrick (@DonWettrick)

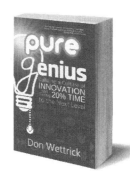

For far too long, schools have been bastions of boredom, killers of creativity, and way too comfortable with compliance and conformity. In *Pure Genius*, Don Wettrick explains how collaboration—with experts, students, and other educators—can help you create interesting, and even life-changing, opportunities for learning. Wettrick's book inspires and equips educators with a systematic blueprint for teaching innovation in any school.

140 Twitter Tips for Educators

Get Connected, Grow Your Professional
Learning Network, and Reinvigorate Your Career

By Brad Currie, Billy Krakower, and Scott Rocco
(@bradmcurrie, @wkrakower, @ScottRRocco)

Whatever questions you have about education or about how you can be even better at your job, you'll find ideas, resources, and a vibrant network of professionals ready to help you on Twitter. In *140 Twitter Tips for Educators*, #Satchat hosts and founders of Evolving Educators, Brad Currie, Billy Krakower, and Scott Rocco, offer step-by-step instructions to help you master the basics of Twitter, build an online following, and become a Twitter rock star.

Ditch That Textbook

Free Your Teaching and Revolutionize
Your Classroom

By Matt Miller (@jmattmiller)

Textbooks are symbols of centuries-old education. They're often outdated as soon as they hit students' desks. Acting "by the textbook" implies compliance and a lack of creativity. It's time to ditch those textbooks—and those textbook assumptions about learning! In *Ditch That Textbook*, teacher and blogger Matt Miller encourages educators to throw out meaningless, pedestrian teaching and learning practices. He empowers them to evolve and improve on old, standard teaching methods. *Ditch That Textbook* is a support system, toolbox, and manifesto to help educators free their teaching and revolutionize their classrooms.

How Much Water Do We Have?

5 Success Principles for Conquering Any Challenge and Thriving in Times of Change

by Pete Nunweiler with Kris Nunweiler

In *How Much Water Do We Have?* Pete Nunweiler identifies five key elements—information, planning, motivation, support, and leadership—that are necessary for the success of any goal, life transition, or challenge. Referring to these elements as the 5 Waters of Success, Pete explains that, like the water we drink, you need them to thrive in today's rapidly paced world. If you're feeling stressed out, overwhelmed, or uncertain at work or at home, pause and look for the signs of dehydration. Learn how to find, acquire, and use the 5 Waters of Success—so you can share them with your team and family members.

Instant Relevance

Using Today's Experiences to Teach Tomorrow's Lessons

By Denis Sheeran (@MathDenisNJ)

Every day, students in schools around the world ask the question, "When am I ever going to use this in real life?" In *Instant Relevance*, author and keynote speaker Denis Sheeran equips you to create engaging lessons *from* experiences and events that matter to your students. Learn how to help your students see meaningful connections between the real world and what they learn in the classroom—because that's when learning sticks.

The Classroom Chef

Sharpen Your Lessons. Season Your Classes. Make Math Meaningful.

By John Stevens and Matt Vaudrey
(@Jstevens009, @MrVaudrey)

In *The Classroom Chef*, math teachers and instructional coaches John Stevens and Matt Vaudrey share their secret recipes, ingredients, and tips for serving up lessons that engage students and help them "get" math. You can use these ideas and methods as-is, or better yet, tweak them and create your own enticing educational meals. The message the authors share is that, with imagination and preparation, every teacher can be a classroom chef.

Start. Right. Now.

Teach and Lead for Excellence

By Todd Whitaker, Jeff Zoul, and Jimmy Casas
(@ToddWhitaker, @Jeff_Zoul, @casas_jimmy)

In their work leading up to *Start. Right. Now.*, Todd Whitaker, Jeff Zoul, and Jimmy Casas studied educators from across the nation and discovered four key behaviors of excellence: Excellent leaders and teachers *Know the Way, Show the Way, Go the Way, and Grow Each Day*. If you are ready to take the first step toward excellence, this motivating book will put you on the right path.

The Writing on the Classroom Wall

How Posting Your Most Passionate Beliefs about Education Can Empower Your Students, Propel Your Growth, and Lead to a Lifetime of Learning

By Steve Wyborney (@SteveWyborney)

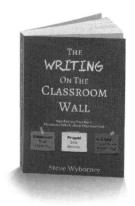

In *The Writing on the Classroom Wall*, Steve Wyborney explains how posting and discussing Big Ideas can lead to deeper learning. You'll learn why sharing your ideas will sharpen and refine them. You'll also be encouraged to know that the Big Ideas you share don't have to be profound to make a profound impact on learning. In fact, Steve explains, it's okay if some of your ideas fall *off* the wall. What matters most is sharing them.

LAUNCH

Using Design Thinking to Boost Creativity and Bring Out the Maker in Every Student

By John Spencer and A.J. Juliani
(@spencerideas, @ajjuliani)

Something happens in students when they define themselves as *makers* and *inventors* and *creators*. They discover powerful skills—problem-solving, critical thinking, and imagination—that will help them shape the world's future ... *our* future. In *LAUNCH*, John Spencer and A.J. Juliani provide a process that can be incorporated into every class at every grade level ... even if you don't consider yourself a "creative teacher." And if you dare to innovate and view creativity as an essential skill, you will empower your students to change the world—starting right now.

Kids Deserve It!

*Pushing Boundaries and Challenging
Conventional Thinking*

By Todd Nesloney and Adam Welcome
(@TechNinjaTodd, @awelcome)

In *Kids Deserve It!*, Todd and Adam encourage you to think big and make learning fun and meaningful for students. Their high-tech, high-touch, and highly engaging practices will inspire you to take risks, shake up the status quo, and be a champion for your students. While you're at it, you just might rediscover why you became an educator in the first place.

Escaping the School Leader's Dunk Tank

How to Prevail When Others Want to See You Drown

By Rebecca Coda and Rick Jetter
(@RebeccaCoda, @RickJetter)

No school leader is immune to the effects of discrimination, bad politics, revenge, or ego-driven coworkers. These kinds of dunk-tank situations can make an educator's life miserable. By sharing real-life stories and insightful research, the authors (who are dunk-tank survivors themselves) equip school leaders with the practical knowledge and emotional tools necessary to survive and, better yet, avoid getting "dunked."

Your School Rocks...So Tell People!

*Passionately Pitch and Promote the
Positives Happening on Your Campus*

By Ryan McLane and Eric Lowe
(@McLane_Ryan, @EricLowe21)

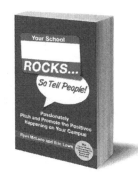

Great things are happening in your school every day. The problem is, no one beyond your school walls knows about them. School principals Ryan McLane and Eric Lowe want to help you get the word out! In *Your School Rocks ... So Tell People!*, McLane and Lowe offer more than seventy immediately actionable tips along with easy-to-follow instructions and links to video tutorials. This practical guide will equip you to create an effective and manageable communication strategy using social media tools. Learn how to keep your students' families and community connected, informed, and excited about what's going on in your school.

Teaching Math with Google Apps

50 G Suite Activities

By Alice Keeler and Diana Herrington
(@AliceKeeler, @mathdiana)

Google Apps give teachers the opportunity to interact with students in a more meaningful way than ever before, while G Suite empowers students to be creative, critical thinkers who collaborate as they explore and learn. In *Teaching Math with Google Apps*, educators Alice Keeler and Diana Herrington demonstrate fifty different ways to bring math classes to the twenty-first century with easy-to-use technology.

Table Talk Math

A Practical Guide for Bringing Math into Everyday Conversations

By John Stevens (@Jstevens009)

Making math part of families' everyday conversations is a powerful way to help children and teens learn to love math. In *Table Talk Math*, John Stevens offers parents (and teachers!) ideas for initiating authentic, math-based conversations that will get kids to notice and be curious about all the numbers, patterns, and equations in the world around them.

Shift This!

How to Implement Gradual Changes for MASSIVE Impact in Your Classroom

By Joy Kirr (@JoyKirr)

Establishing a student-led culture that isn't focused on grades and homework but on individual responsibility and personalized learning may seem like a daunting task—especially if you think you have to do it all at once. But significant change is possible, sustainable, and even easy when it happens little by little. In *Shift This!* educator and speaker Joy Kirr explains how to make gradual shifts—in your thinking, teaching, and approach to classroom design—that will have a massive impact in your classroom. Make the first shift today!

Unmapped Potential

An Educator's Guide to Lasting Change

By Julie Hasson and Missy Lennard (@PPrincipals)

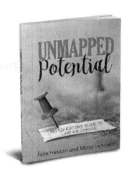

No matter where you are in your educational career, chances are you have, at times, felt overwhelmed and overworked. Maybe you feel that way right now. If so, you aren't alone. But the more important news is that things can get better! You simply need the right map to guide you from frustrated to fulfilled. *Unmapped Potential* offers advice and practical strategies to help you find your unique path to becoming the kind of educator—the kind of person—you want to be.

Social LEADia

Moving Students from Digital Citizenship to Digital Leadership

By Jennifer Casa-Todd (@JCasaTodd)

Equipping students for their future begins by helping them become digital leaders now. In our networked society, students need to learn how to leverage social media to connect to people, passions, and opportunities to grow and make a difference. *Social LEADia* addresses the need to shift the conversations at school and at home from digital citizenship to digital leadership.

Shattering the Perfect Teacher Myth

6 Truths That Will Help You THRIVE as an Educator

By Aaron Hogan (@aaron_hogan)

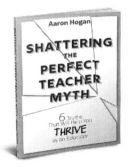

The idyllic myth of the perfect teacher perpetuates unrealistic expectations that erode self-confidence and set teachers up for failure. Author and educator Aaron Hogan is on a mission to shatter the myth of the perfect teacher by equipping educators with strategies that help them shift out of survival mode and THRIVE.

Spark Learning

3 Keys to Embracing the Power of Student Curiosity

By Ramsey Musallam (@ramusallam)

Inspired by his popular TED Talk "3 Rules to Spark Learning," this book combines brain science research, proven teaching methods, and Ramsey's personal story to empower you to improve your students' learning experiences by inspiring inquiry and harnessing its benefits. If you want to engage students in more interesting and effective learning, this is the book for you.

The Four O'Clock Faculty

A Rogue Guide to Revolutionizing Professional Development

By Rich Czyz (@RACzyz)

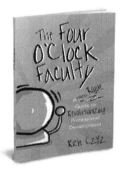

Author Rich Czyz is on a mission to revolutionize professional learning for all educators. In *The Four O'Clock Faculty*, Rich identifies ways to make PD meaningful, efficient, and, above all, personally relevant. This book is a practical guide that reveals why some PD is so awful and what you can do to change the model for the betterment of you and your colleagues.

BRING MATT MILLER
TO YOUR SCHOOL,
DISTRICT, OR EVENT!

When you hire Matt Miller to speak, you're putting more than a decade of "in the trenches" teaching experience in the hands of your teachers. He has delivered keynotes, workshops, and concurrent conference sessions to thousands of teachers about technology and its thoughtful integration. He's spoken at International Society for Technology in Education (ISTE), Michigan Association for Computer Users in Learning (MACUL), the TeachTechPlay Conference in Melbourne, Australia, and dozens and dozens of school districts and schools. Here's what people are saying:

> "Matt's call to 'Ditch That Textbook' couldn't be a timelier message for today's educators and should be an anthem for schools hoping to become more relevant for today's learners. His challenge to replace outdated, traditional practices with more innovative methods is inspiring."
>
> —GEORGE PHILHOWER, ASSISTANT SUPERINTENDENT, WESTERN WAYNE SCHOOLS, PERSHING, INDIANA

> "Matt's presentations have been a homerun with our faculty and received rave reviews from all teachers and administrators. We were so pleased; we've already asked him back!"
>
> —SUSAN DRUMM, INSTRUCTIONAL TECHNOLOGY COACH, HAMILTON SOUTHEASTERN SCHOOLS, FISHERS, INDIANA

"This is the best hands-on tech workshop for all levels teachers. Whether you are just curious about introducing a little tech into the classroom or want to jump in full force, this workshop can lead you in the right direction!"

—**VALERIE GARCIA**, TEACHER, ANNA INDEPENDENT
SCHOOL DISTRICT, ANNA, TEXAS

"I had a great time. Matt made the day quite enjoyable. I am leaving with a great toolbox of ideas to use with technology!"

—**TROY SMITH**, TEACHER, UNIFIED SCHOOL
DISTRICT 385, ANDOVER, KANSAS

Popular presentation topics include:
Ditch That Textbook keynote speech

Ditch That Homework workshop, breakout session or keynote speech

Google Genius: Practical Google Activities for Class Tomorrow

Connecting Classrooms to the World with Skype and Google Hangouts

The Digital PIRATE: Tech Like a PIRATE

For more information, go to
DitchThatTextbook.com/WorkWithMatt

ABOUT THE AUTHORS

MATT MILLER is an educator, blogger, presenter, and key-note speaker with more than ten years of teaching experience in public education. After trying to follow traditional practices and "teaching by the textbook" for a few years, he chose to take the less-traveled, textbook-free path. His journey led to technology-inspired custom learning activities. He and his students have liked the results—a lot.

He wrote the book *Ditch That Textbook: Free Your Teaching and Revolutionize Your Classroom*, which has sold more than twenty thousand print and digital copies. It encourages educators to ditch their traditional "textbook" activities and mindsets toward education with newer innovative ones. It has spurred a Twitter community—#DitchBook—where educators share ideas and encouragement 24/7. It's also home to a weekly Twitter chat on Thursday nights at 10 Eastern/7 Pacific.

Matt's commitment to excellence in teaching and technology integration was recognized by WTHI-TV in Terre Haute, Indiana, with the Golden Apple Award. He was named a Bammy! Top to Watch in 2016 and one of the top ten influencers in educational technology and elearning worldwide by Onalytica. He also has the distinction of being a Google Certified Innovator.

He has reached countless educators around the world as a popular author, blogger, and education speaker. With tens of thousands of subscribers and visitors from more than two hundred countries, Matt's blog, DitchThatTextbook.com, is a well-respected source of ideas and insights about educational technology and creative teaching.

He is a proud graduate of Indiana State University (Go Sycamores!) and is living the dream with a wife, three kids, a mortgage, and two dogs.

Connect with him... he lives for it!

@jmattmiller / #DitchBook

facebook.com/DitchThatTextbook

youtube.com/DitchThatTextbook

pinterest.com/DitchThatTxt

matt@DitchThatTextbook.com

ALICE KEELER is a mom of five children. She taught high school math for fourteen years and currently teaches in the credential program at California State University Fresno. She is a Google Certified Innovator and Microsoft Innovative Educator. Alice has a master's degree in Educational Media Design and Technology and frequently blogs about teaching on her top ranking edtech website alicekeeler.com. Alice co-authored the books *50 Things You Can Do With Google Classroom*; *50 Things to Go Further with Google Classroom: A Student-Centered Approach*; *Teaching Math with Google Apps*; *Google Apps for Littles*; and *Ditch that Homework.*

Made in the USA
Lexington, KY
28 July 2017